CARRY O

First published in 2008 by

WOODFIELD PUBLISHING LTD
Bognor Regis ~ West Sussex ~ England ~ PO21 5EL
www.woodfieldpublishing.com

© Edward Cartner, 2008

ISBN 1-84683-065-6

Carry On Corporal

*A humorous look at life
in the Royal Air Force*

EDWARD CARTNER

Woodfield

Woodfield Publishing Ltd

Woodfield House ~ Babsham Lane ~ Bognor Regis ~ West Sussex ~ PO21 5EL
telephone 01243 821234 ~ **e-mail** enquiries@woodfieldpublishing.co.uk

Interesting and informative books on a variety of subjects

For full details of all our published titles, visit our website at
www.woodfieldpublishing.co.uk

~ CONTENTS ~

Introduction

A guest at my daughter's wedding in Hong Kong was a Gurkha soldier who told me with unaffected pride that he was a corporal. No diffidence. He did not say 'just a corporal'. He *was* a corporal.

And quite rightly too. That soldier held honourable status; the first of the NCO ranks and frequently the ones who have to make things happen.

Of all NCO groups, I served closely with corporals least. So – and doubtless much to their collective relief – they rarely had to correct my well-meaning but frequently ineffectual interference. Well, at least not in my presence, that is.

It is curious that corporals appear less than others in film.

Bully-boy sergeants, yes.

Silly-ass officers, certainly.

But corporals?

If that is true, I wonder why?

Whatever the reason, I enjoyed the professional company of many NCOs – corporals, sergeants and warrant officers alike. I really did try my utmost not to spoil too many of their days – although the reader may find the odd scene in these tales to disprove that.

Edward Cartner
Plymouth 2008

About the Author

Edward Cartner began his working life teaching English and Physical Education in Northumberland, but was commissioned into the Royal Air Force in 1964. He was to serve for nearly thirty years in a variety of appointments – half them as a parachute instructor – before retiring from the very office in Central London where he had been interviewed for entry to the Service. He lives in the West Country with his wife. They have two married daughters.

1. TAKING THE SHILLING

A favourite uncle – he had, according to family legend, been 'busted' repeatedly from Lance Corporal – thought I was crazy.

'What?' he cried. 'Join up? You must be mad!'

Then my college tutor had warned, 'Keep mum until you graduate. The Principal dislikes the military.'

However, my bride of barely two months – with most to lose – simply accepted my plan as part of life's great adventure.

'Let's break away,' she said. 'I can't wait to see the world.' (Decades later she was still waiting, but that is another story.)

So, having had non-existent prospects of becoming an officer in the Army a few years earlier, it was supremely ironic that the Royal Air Force offered commissioned service to those with the very qualification I had just acquired.

There were, of course, a few hoops to jump through first.

Having innocently assumed that my multi-page application would open all doors immediately, I then fretted anxiously while the system no doubt ground through hundreds of other petitions. Eventually, I was invited to attend interviews at an RAF station whose famous wartime name alone was enough to brace any young man's shoulders. The place was just south of London, but from my view (well north of Newcastle) seemed closer to France than anywhere else.

The selection procedure would extend over the last three days of 1963, including a final interview in London, and my excitement obscured the significance of those dates. Only my wife remained calm enough to note that the rail warrant included a return journey.

About 40 candidates arrived at the selection centre on a Sunday afternoon and the processing began immediately. A central waiting area offered safe haven between activities, but our numbers began to dwindle almost at once. Those, it seemed, who had arrived in motorbike leathers, unshaven chins and jeans, simply disappeared; our diminished band of tweed jackets and pressed slacks huddled closer.

Then followed an intimate medical going-over, after which further gaps appeared, giving rise to the rumour that tattoos and dirty fingernails provoked rejection.

In our six-man barrack block accommodation that evening there was little conversation before 'lights out'. We were total strangers, clearly in competition one with another and stunned by the fearsome attrition rate.

On Day Two we wore large numbers on coloured bibs, thus confirming to the few 'old hands' that joining-up would quickly reduce us to mere ciphers.

During group discussions staff members provoked us into whatever opinions we judged safe. Were *Daily Star* and *Sporting Times* readers culled here? We never knew, but there were another half-dozen or so empty places at the lunch table.

Practical leadership exercises, in a hangar full of 50-gallon oil drums, planks of wood and lots of rope, gave me some hope. I had spent my teenage years sailing boats and building Boy Scout bridges; at last I felt nearly at home.

We returned to the holding area. A few more souls departed.

Soon we were called individually into inner sanctums where, resigned to the evening train north, I was pleasantly surprised to be questioned kindly on my motives for joining the RAF. In my demoralised state I had no sensible answer, so another surprise was an invitation to await instructions for the morning session in Central London.

In the mess hall I joined another of my group. It mattered little that his name escaped me; all candidates had taken to using their bib numbers anyway. To get too personal might condemn you to the 'disappeared'.

'Hello, Number Three,' he said. 'What day it is?'

'Er ... Tuesday?'

'Aye,' he agreed mournfully, in a thickening Scottish accent. 'And Hogmanay as well.'

Now the date's true meaning hit home and I took my first taste of military mischief.

As a Northumbrian, I had known nothing other than extended jollification at the year's end. On New Year's Eve there was dancing in the streets. In the morning neither shops nor banks opened and we took our hangovers to cheer the runners pounding the Great North Road.

Now, with a very sad Jock, I was in a part of the Kingdom that had yet to recognise the festival at all. It was enough to make a fellow disobey orders long before becoming subject to military discipline.

No other from our group appeared and we ate alone, amidst many empty places, just like a battered bomber squadron in a war film.

'You finished here now?' Number Six asked, after a long silence.

'I think so, but I've an interview in London tomorrow morning.'

'Aye, me too … some place called Aylesbury … where the hell's that?'

'Well, let's see the New Year in properly.' I offered. 'I've not missed one since I was fifteen.'

There were none of our fellows in the candidates' bar either – we appeared to be the sole survivors. The barman said he was closing in ten minutes' time – at nine o'clock, to our astonishment – but as it was New Year's Eve he could stretch the rules and allow us two small bottles of beer each. Where we drank it was not his business.

Back in the deserted dormitory, between haunting pibrochs on Number Six's chanter, we sipped our beer in a miserly fashion and reviewed our progress.

Had we been accepted?

What did all these empty beds signify?

Two days ago, forty-odd young hopefuls had arrived, now only two remained. Who would 'get the chop' in the morning?

'Happy New Year, Number Three,' toasted my companion at about ten thirty. 'Good luck for tomorrow.'

I had not been in bed so early on New Year's Eve since … well, as I said … since I was fifteen.

In the morning I took a solitary breakfast in the candidates' mess hall, then, after much map consultation, found my way by bus and train into central London. How could these streams of grey-faced city workers not understand that it was New Year's morning?

My interview was in a dismal office block in Holborn. Naturally, being a rustic from the Frozen North, I pronounced it *Holl-Born*. There I discussed this and that with a City-suited officer, whose eminence was only revealed by his office-door name board. He released me to King's Cross station well before lunch, but gave no hint about my success or otherwise.

'We'll have to think again,' I summarised despondently to my wife, after a New Year's Day spent largely on public transport.

Three weeks later, an anonymous letter signified success.

Sir, it began, *I am commanded by the Air Council to inform you …*

The brevity was anticlimactic, but no matter. I was *in*.

I had taken the shilling.

Twenty-nine years later – my wife still awaiting worldwide travel – I was in the same dismal office block in Holborn again (having learned, meanwhile, to pronounce it *Hoe-bun*).

Nothing had changed. The corridors of power were just as gloomy, the curtains as dusty. An office-door name board revealed some small eminence.

Dear God! The City-suited inhabitant was me.

There was one consolation.

During my years of service, civilisation had spread southwards, so thankfully I would not be offering the Queen's shilling to any hapless young officer candidates on a New Year's Morning.

2. ORDERLY DOG

An older and worldlier officer pushed me aside as I hesitantly tapped on the Adjutant's door to report for my first period of Orderly Officer duty.

'Learn one thing now, son,' he advised, brusquely. 'Officers don't stand around in corridors.'

With that, he led me into the Great Man's presence, gave a sketchy salute and a breezy, 'Morning, Don; here's a new sprog for your duty list.'

I saluted carefully, as illustrated in the drill book, while my escort lolled carelessly on a chair.

'Deal with the boy,' he conceded graciously. 'I need to talk about next week's cricket.'

The Adjutant seemed harassed, belying rank and influence beyond my dreams.

'Yes?' he demanded, testily, from behind swirls of cigarette smoke.

'It's about my Orderly Officer duty tomorrow, sir,' I began. 'Is this where I sign ...'

'Yes it is.' He consulted a list. 'You're new, aren't you? When did you commission?'

'Only last...'

'Never mind. You'll soon get the hang of things. Here are your orders. Sign here.' With an airy wave he signalled my dismissal and turned to coffee and cricket.

It seemed the wrong time to remind him that we cadets had been assured that many stations allowed a new officer to understudy someone who had performed the duty at least once before and that a period of 'settling-in' to one's new role in life was normal.

There could be no arguing, however. These were times when everybody knew who the Adjutant was, and that, in the direct name of the station commander, he issued requests to many senior officers and orders and instructions to all juniors. It was a time-honoured military appointment, so I had better just get on with things.

The Duty Book then spelled out in stern phrases what I was to do before and after 'working hours': wear 'best blue' uniform, complete with snappy 'OO' armband in fetching red on black; remain on the station; salute the ensign.

Attached to the routine orders book was an additional instruction requiring me to conduct a surprise check on the Dry Ration Store. It was a puzzle. What and where was the Dry Ration Store?

In a casual hypothetical, 'what if' sort of way, I mentioned this to the bar steward after dinner and, despite his cheeky grin, got the answer I needed.

Then I recalled how the episode of the 'Puff-Puff Machine' had been the talk of the place only two weeks earlier.

Evidently, the Orderly Officer, making a night-hours check on the armoury, had come across a vat of busily-bubbling tar. Seeing hot, unattended machinery churning around so close to the explosives store, the Orderly Dog considered he had no choice but to ferret about until he found the 'off' switch.

Unfortunately, the tar boiler belonged to contractors who were on site to seal the many flat roofs about the place. Having got their gloop warmed to the consistency of black treacle, it was normal practice to leave it simmering over-night, the better to make an early start the next day. A night watchman would appear occasionally to see that all was well. Unfortunately, our military guardian appeared just as the tar man was taking a glass in the Airmen's Club.

In the morning the Orderly Officer had proudly reported his initiative, but had no answer to the Adjutant's angry questions about how the workmen were expected to begin their new day with a semi-solid ball of lukewarm bitumen.

Such tales were enough to make a young lad quake with the fearsome responsibility of it all, so I resolved to ask as many questions of the specialists in the Dry Ration Store as I could.

In the morning I arrived at the store, in company with a senior NCO of the catering branch. None of the store's inhabitants appeared too surprised to see me, despite my 'secret' Orderly Officer instructions being confirmed barely an hour earlier. Two civilians in khaki dustcoats steered me, with a series of meaningful glances, through an apparently random choice as I ticked off my check sheet. Sacks of flour, drums of salt and large square tins of something called 'biscuits dry tack' were all paraded in good order.

The store was clean and the contents matched my check-list. Furthermore, I was humbled to note, they were giving the young officer every assistance in making an efficient check.

As I turned to leave, a waist-high open sack of yellow split peas caught my eye.

'Goodness,' I marvelled innocently, taking a tentative handful. 'How long does it take to get through *that* lot?'

'Blow me!' cried one of the men, pushing me aside. 'Just how did *that* get in there?' And he delved elbow-deep into the lentils to pull out a whole cured ham, white mutton cloth and all. 'Must have fallen off the shelf, sir, and sunk in.'

'Christ!' muttered the catering sergeant and rushed out of the storeroom. He returned with the Catering Officer, long before I had reconciled my clipboard with the facts before my eyes and remarked how odd it was that meat and dry rations were stored together.

'Okay,' said the caterer, yet another officer senior to me. 'I'll take it from here...'

The Adjutant was almost comradely when I signed off from duty. 'You did well there, son,' he allowed. 'Must have X-ray eyes. The caterers have been trying to sort that out for some time.'

What I had stumbled into was a mystery, but the Adjutant seemed pleased. Perhaps it had been an on-the-job training exercise?

I did notice, however, that subsequent Orderly Dog duties became more straightforward.

The word must have got about somehow.

3. YOU WILL BE ESCORTED, SIR

'There are three certain causes of an officer's downfall,' one of our more eccentric mentors at the officer cadet unit told us. 'Keep clear of them and nothing much else should bother you in this man's air force.

It was an intriguing introduction to his lecture on professional deportment, and we looked at each other in wonderment.

'And they are...' he continued enigmatically, 'losing state secrets, messing about with other officers' wives and...' a dramatic pause here ... 'carelessness with public money.'

It was a solemn lesson, requiring each point to be considered in turn.

I was too junior to be entrusted with anything more secret than the name of the CO's dog. As for women, I was having enough difficulty meeting the domestic standards set by my bride of less than a year to consider taking on any more trouble. And money? What little I had was largely spent on the aforementioned domestic standards, so carelessness, public or otherwise would be impossible.

Soon the training system spat us into the real world with the promise that hiding behind our specialist procedures would not prevent exposure to the strange ways of other departments. We were all part of one Air Force and it was not long before I was 'volunteered' for extra duties.

I was to take a pay parade and so *probable negligence with public money* loomed large immediately. I was further alarmed to learn that troops without bank accounts paraded before an officer to receive their wages in cash over a table.

'Worry not,' I was told. It was a simple well-established procedure.

'You,' the experts told me, 'go to the accounts office, where you sign for the accumulated pay of the squad in question. Then they form up on parade and you pay them.'

The men were used to it, the averred, and anyway, the procedure was all 'in the book'.

Discreet reading gave me the gist of the business. The men would form up as I sat at a table, behind a large pile of banknotes; an NCO would order each man forward at the salute, I would consult a list and publicly count out the man's due. After further saluting, the grateful recipient would march back to his place in the ranks.

Yes, it appeared simple enough, but what about that *carelessness with public money* warning? When did the Queen's money become theirs? Would there be time to check the arithmetic between the sergeant's shouts?

Eventually I presented myself at the station pay office to sign for the nominal roll and money of those to be paid by me that day. The cash, of course, matched exactly the sum of the individual payments and, by some magic well beyond my understanding, each of these had been calculated to a whole figure payable in folding money.

The civilian pay clerk, who was notorious for his contempt towards junior officers of my unit, waited with cynical weariness as I counted and re-counted. These were pre-Pound and Fifty Pence coin days, so all the notes became well mixed until, in mild panic, I accepted responsibility for the equivalent of several weeks-worth of my own pay.

Meanwhile, I had had a brainwave. The pay parade was to be at a satellite airfield that we used as a dropping zone for trainee parachutists so, in a bold variation of the book, I would *parachute in* with the money.

'I've got a plane to catch,' I quipped to the man, as I turned to leave. He seemed unimpressed.

'Your vehicle and escort are ready at the front, *sir*.'

'No need, thank you. I know these men, so I have arranged to jump in. I'll stuff it down the front of my overall. The parachute harness will keep it tight.'

This was the way to demonstrate to these desk-wallahs that I was back on my own territory again! But rather than expressing awestruck admiration for this heroic interpretation of the rules, the wretched man simply reverted to a stuffy repetition of the procedure.

'That's not allowed, *Sir*,' he continued, with increasing emphasis on the '*Sir*'. 'Because you're going off station, *Sir*, we have to use a special vehicle. It has a strong box bolted to the floor, *Sir*, and there's an escort as well as the driver.'

Thus it was that I found myself on the 20-mile journey to my parade – money, official briefcase, floor safe and all.

My teenage protector hefted his ironbound pickaxe helve. Who would he hit first if we were attacked, I pondered? The robbers or me?

And indeed it was simple. The dozen or so men formed up neatly and all was in accordance with good order and military discipline until the last man marched forward.

'Four five eight Jones, Sah!' he announced loudly, in the approved manner.

I consulted my list.

'Twenty Pounds ten Shillings,' I declared confidently.

I was getting used to this.

The last of the money was handed over.

Jones picked it up, gave it a surreptitious once-over, signed, saluted and returned to the ranks, all in one fluid ballet of foot drill.

My sigh of relief died at birth. Two crisp One Pound notes lurked with my completed nominal roll.

'Permission to dismiss the men, sir?'

It was the sergeant, the one really in charge.

'Er … can you get them to check their money, please?'

'Well… okay sir, but they should have checked it at the table.'

The man was forcing me to reveal all.

'Yes, of course, but you see …' and I gave him covert sight of the offending notes.

'Ah, I see, sir,' he said, with a happy wink and set the men to counting.

There were no complaints from the men and they were dismissed.

During the return to base – still menaced by my escort – I chewed over the *carelessness with* warning heard so long ago. Was my burgeoning career about to founder on my shoddy arithmetic?

Honesty seemed the best policy, so I made an abject confession to the clerk.

'It happens occasionally,' he sniffed. 'Better to be up than down, I suppose. Presumably you got everybody to double check?' His contempt was having a field day, not a single *'sir'*, genuine or otherwise.

A dignified silence seemed best, but he had the last word as I turned to go.

'By the way, *sir*, if you've the time, the Warrant Officer would like a word about that parachuting idea.'

And so a little procession ascended into the upper reaches of the accounts section. The clerk bore in triumph my nominal roll and the errant pound notes as clear evidence of my cavalier approach to public money.

I might laugh off the parachuting-in-with-the-money idea as youthful gung-ho enthusiasm, but the surplus, despite all the counting and signatures, was something else – and no junior officer was going to win an argument with a warrant officer, especially one on his own ground.

The clerk launched into his condemnation at once, but was quickly obliged to agree that banknotes had been known to stick together, Accounts Clerks had been known to miscount and that the officer had double-checked with the men.

Fifteen love to me.

'No doubt all will be well on that side, but I would like a private word with the officer, please,' the warrant officer concluded, in easy dismissal.

'Mr Smith mentioned your jumping-in-with-the-money idea,' he continued, with a grin, as the outraged clerk closed the door. 'But let's deal with the surplus first…'

I tensed, as courts martial images blossomed again.

'It's as he said,' the Warrant continued, to my relief. 'It happens now and again and we'll sort it out. The parachuting idea, however, was different. The rules and common sense are very protective of public money. Just think what might have happened if you'd been injured ... or your parachute failed ... or ...'

'But that was unlikely,' I interrupted. 'At least I know what I'm doing there.'

'Maybe, but my neck would have been on the block and I'm not having my pension put at risk by some daft young officer.'

I was in real trouble now, and quite properly was being instructed as if by a Dutch uncle.

What was I thinking about? This man wasn't Dutch at all; he was my father's brother-in-law.

'It is right that I should guide young officers,' the Warrant continued, 'and I have been leading you since you were a little boy, but not this time. They used to talk about three things that could wreck a career,' he continued. 'Did you ever hear that?'

'Oh yes.'

'Then my advice is to remember them.'

'I will indeed, Uncle George. Thank you.'

4.   A BOY AMONG MEN

Despite a pocketful of diplomas, my employment as a teacher was short. To the astonishment of all, I joined the Royal Air Force after serving only two school terms.

A colleague marked my departure with a solemn warning.

'Here,' he said, lugubriously, 'you have been a man among boys. There you will be a boy among men.'

His counsel seemed irrelevant at the officer cadet unit. There, every entrant from civilian life seemed boyish, but with our wiser brothers, who had done time in the ranks, we formed a symbiotic self-protection society. They taught us how to press our uniforms and keep out of trouble; we helped them with their rusty classroom techniques.

Later, in the real Air Force, 'infancy' gave some protection and my conversion from 'boy' to 'man' only really began after training as a specialist.

And all thanks to one man...

Sergeant Franks, as large as his loud regional accent suggested, was a parachute instructor of the 'old school'. His mantra of *mind over matter – we don't mind and you don't matter* – when applied to an anxious trainee, was a worrying new concept to newly-qualified college-boy officers.

Our relationship began one morning on board the transport to the training jump area.

'By 'eck, Mr Cartner,' declared Franks. 'That's reet good baccy.'

'Indeed, Sergeant, er...' I was unsure of his name, but a touch of commissioned largesse might set the tone. 'Would you care for a fill?'

'You're a proper gentleman. I'll not say no,' he replied, whereupon he produced a small plant-pot masquerading as a Meerschaum pipe and purloined the entire contents of my tobacco pouch – Balkan Sobranie it was, and right on the upper limits of my pay band.

It was a powerful lesson and I quickly developed great sympathy for a friend's view. Franks was a fine instructor – reputedly the tough Paras ate from his hand – but what was needed was a box to keep him in out of working hours.

Later, on appointment to more operational parachute duties, I was dismayed to inherit pastoral responsibilities for Sergeant Franks, who had preceded me. My conversion from boy to man had been doing well, but this threatened a setback.

One Monday, after returning from an extended detachment, I went into my unit to request a couple of days leave but was confronted by Franks before I got to the boss.

'Can I 'ave a word, sir?'

It was a rare but encouraging use of my title.

'Very well, come and see me Friday morning.'

'It's a bit urgent. The police have reported me, like.'

Oh Lord, I thought, *bang goes my leave.*

In my office, strewn with unattended paperwork – all as pictured in the best man-management brochures – Franks began a convoluted tale. Two weeks earlier the police had picked him up for drink driving. He'd had 'a couple, mebbe.' His licence carried a Maltese endorsement.

'Sounds like there's not much I can do for you.'

Then his clincher. He had received the 'summons thingy' but it gave the wrong street on the wrong date – and he had someone to prove it.

This was my let-out.

'Well… that's probably your only hope. Bring him into the story.' My recent dream of two days in the bosom of my little family surfaced again. 'Good luck.'

'Can't do that, sir,' he confessed, without a blush. 'It were t'Sergeant Major's wife. We were parked up, having a bit of a cuddle, like. But you're my officer and could write an official letter explaining things. Her name wouldn't come out then.'

'Oh come on, Sergeant Franks!' This unexpected protest inadvertently took me into the realms of 'man among men' and he left abruptly with stage whispers about 'officers never help when you need it'.

I went home to an overstretched domestic list – a wife who thought I had set up home on Salisbury Plain; an un-cooperative heating boiler and (through my own careless-ness) a tiny tot who had recently poured garden creosote over herself.

'Who looks after *us*, love?' I marvelled, despairingly.

'We do,' she said grimly, knee-deep in a throng of little people.

Later that year I was required to supervise a parachute drop on the Isle of Man, in company with Sergeant Franks. A long journey, cramped knee-to-knee in a Land Rover, would hardly allow a traditional officer/man relationship, so there was mutual willingness on both sides to forgive and forget. Also, I had been amazed to learn that the police had not pressed charges against him.

So, with no reference to wives – his, mine, or the sergeant major's – we travelled to Douglas in careful harmony.

In the absence of any service accommodation we lodged in a half-board guesthouse. There was no 'officers'-only' entertainment, so after supper we repaired to the seafront fleshpots and a frantic bar full of holidaymakers.

My plan to ensure equal shares of the beer kitty and consumption was thwarted by an immediate need to make a telephone call. In those pre-mobile phone days it was common when on detached duty to use a public kiosk to contact base for any changes to plan and to get an up-to-date weather forecast. I was confident, however, that drink, kitty and team would survive the new mood of man-to-man trust.

My call took some time, and on return I found a family – parents and two awe-struck teenage girls – all drinking in Frank's every word.

'Ay oop, Eddie,' he cried, 'how's things looking for tomorrow?'

While I struggled for a non-military reply, he continued, with a knowing wink to the mother.

'Like I said, I'm the pilot, he's the navigator. We go back a long way. He's been to get t'weather. Ow's it looking, then?'

The kitty and my beer had gone, so there was only one possible response, and with a nod to the group and a curt 'flight briefing at 0700', I left.

With luck, 'Dad' would turn out to be a real airline pilot and so contribute to Franks' self-dug hole, but it seemed my steady advance to full manhood had suffered another setback.

I knew Franks would be prompt in the morning, but where was that box to put him in at the end of the working day?

In the morning our task was completed without problems and by lunchtime we were on the airstrip, chatting to the aircrew. With unusual diffidence, Sergeant Franks mentioned that he would speak to the aircraft captain ('a mate of mine') and fix up a lift to get him home for his son's sports day.

It was a good shot, but I was triumphantly ahead. Earlier, I had spoken to the crew, hoping to get us on board, but there simply was no room.

'Sorry, boss,' the Loadmaster had said, 'we could take *you*, but not your driver and the Land Rover.'

But no, and despite a delightful image of Franks as a *driver*, I could not allow that. We were a team. We lived and worked together. Where I went, even Franks was obliged to follow.

He was to take his turn at driving, so did not drink on the ferry. I took this as confirmation of my new leadership, but probably he was remembering his drink-driving near miss. Even so, it seemed like a capitulation and, despite his frequent loaded reference to extended duty and school fetes during the wearisome trek from Liverpool to Aldershot, I was content.

There had been times when I thought it would never come about, but my conversion from 'boy' to 'man' seemed almost complete.

5. CARRY ON, CORPORAL

'Delegate!' my mentor cried in exasperation, as I frantically tried to catch the egg, while my near-mutinous colleagues sprawled wetly on the track. 'Learn to delegate!'

My first practical leadership exercise at the officer cadet unit had ended in humiliation – too close to the radioactive 'bomb'; collapse of the improvised remote handling device while fording the brook and loss of the egg downstream.

The flight commander's summary said it all. My briefing had been rushed and incoherent. Only in war films does the leader do everything himself. It had not been my job to tie the many knots involved. What about losing control of my team, who had then wandered off in non-contributory directions? Why had I so obviously lost my sense of humour and temper when everything stalled, literally in mid-stream? Worse by far, by an absence of wise delegation I had failed to direct the skills and enthusiasm of my men to complete the task.

'Delegation is the key to relaxed but effective leadership,' my tutor went on. (The word 'management' had yet to appear in the officer-training lexicon.)

'Tell your troops what the plan is, then stand back a little. Give them some room and a chance to shine. I call it a "Carry on, Corporal" moment. The trick is knowing when it arrives.'

Some of my fellow cadets, who had actually served as corporals, took that theory slightly askance, but for a young lad fresh from civilian life it was an intriguing new concept. In my previous incarnation as a schoolteacher, to 'stand back a little' in a gymnasium full of unruly teenagers in order to 'give them some room' would have been suicidal.

Nonetheless, the lessons learned from our early cadet disasters allowed most of us to survive further exercises until – after much instructors' teeth-sucking – we were released to the 'real' Air Force.

Here, at the bottom of the officers' pecking order, I grew accustomed to my betters standing back after their many delegations of extra and frequently puzzling duty. Gradually, I perceived that in the modern services the daily tasks, and most of the extraordinary ones, were achieved through an un-stated but pervasive blend of all-rubbing-in-together teamwork. My naive perception, that officers 'stood back', never to become personally involved in manual work, was dissolved forever when, along with other juniors, I was tasked one day to clear snow from my share of the airfield taxiway.

'Carry on Corporal' possibilities receded even further when I was posted to a unit where the staff minimum rank was sergeant. There could be no question of upgrading the 'moment' by a rank; at that stage the sergeants had a far better grasp of the job's technicalities than I could ever hope to attain and 'carried on' regardless. Even my boss, although careful to include me, took the real 'nitty-gritty' from the men when required.

Then, after my first promotion, I stood my first night as Station Duty Officer – a sort of stand-in-station-commander during out-of-normal hours that gave me command of a small hierarchy of duty personnel.

My junior, the Orderly Officer, did the running about – checking things, saluting flags, visiting the men's mess hall and the like. An NCO – at least of sergeant rank – commanded the guard, formed by a corporal and a squad of airmen. It was the ultimate stand-back-and-delegate exercise.

Nothing of note occurred until I was in the shower and a mess steward came knocking (the duty bedroom phone was not working). 'Sorry to bother you, sir. There's a call for you at Reception.'

'Yes?' I queried, eventually, easing damp clothing off my back.

'Sorry to bother you, Sir…' It was the Orderly Officer, one so new that he addressed everybody by formal title. 'I think there's a problem with the Guardroom Key Register.'

'Is that so? Then sort it with the Orderly Sergeant.'

It was masterly delegation, giving the young lad a chance to shine. Exactly as taught all those years earlier.

An hour later, just as I sat down to dinner, the telephone beckoned once again.

'Sorry to bother you, Sir…' It was 'guess who' again. 'There's definitely a set of keys missing.'

'You've double-checked the register against the authorised names, I presume?'

'Not yet, Sir,' the lad said abjectly.

'Well, do it now.'

More superb delegation, even though, but unknown to the youngster, that exhausted my knowledge of key security.

At half past ten the Orderly Officer called again.

'I've done that check,' he offered anxiously. 'The missing keys are for the armoury, but I think we're...'

I cut him short. Suddenly this was no time for hapless explanation. 'I'll be over right away,' I snapped.

Of all the keys to lose, they had to be for the most sensitive building on the station! And on my watch too!

My period of 'standing back' was abruptly over.

At the Guardroom, the lad greeted me with some relief.

'Show me the key register,' I demanded, tersely. 'Who signed out the keys this morning? Is it an authorised signature? Has anybody actually checked the building?'

My blizzard of angry demands galvanised the Orderly Officer, who rushed out with a couple of airmen.

'Sorry, sir,' he called. 'On my way now.'

No amount of *sorry sir* could obscure that I was running out of ideas and control.

The Orderly Sergeant was entangled in a sweaty minefield of register checks.

'Leave that for the Duty Corporal,' I ordered angrily. 'Where is he, by the way?'

'Sorry, sir... I stood in for him ... he had some work to catch up on.'

As if on cue, a Corporal entered. He carried a large bunch of keys. 'Hello sir,' he said. He was the first that evening not to begin with *sorry, sir.*

'This is Corporal Jones,' the sergeant reported. 'He's back on duty now.'

'Excuse me sir,' Jones said, 'I'll just sign in these keys.' Of all those present only he appeared confident about anything.

'Are those the *armoury* keys?' I asked slowly.

'That's right, sir. I work there ... had a spot of catching-up to do ... kept the keys from sign-out this morning.' He looked towards the Sergeant. 'Is there a problem?'

'Not at all,' I interrupted, recognising both my saviour and the long-awaited *moment*. Duties had been delegated; chances to shine were on offer; with luck, even the hapless young officer would return without crashing the Land Rover.

Only one requirement remained.

'Carry on, Corporal,' I delegated, magnanimously.

6. BIRTHDAY BOY

The demands of armed forces duty usually limited any birthday celebration to immediate family – and possibly a modest round of drinks bought for one's closest cronies. Otherwise, the Great Day was absorbed into the current preoccupation and the memory of it lost forever, this being a right and proper inevitability.

'Three Para are going to Malta,' my CO announced early in my military youth. 'Sort yourself passage out there and see what they need from us.'

He meant 3rd Battalion The Parachute Regiment. *Needing from us* meant parachute training – that being our business – and I had a reasonable idea where Malta was.

The correct response was, 'Very good, sir,' a smart salute and about turn, all followed by purposeful 'sorting' , but I had a host of concerns – *When? How long for? Who with? Does the battalion know I'm coming? It's a bit sudden...*

My boss's response, of course, was a repeated expectation of quick reaction on my part.

I arrived at the departure air terminal within a day or two to find that short-notice, an absence of advance paperwork and what the Air Movements staff saw as 'non-standard baggage' would hinder my smooth progress.

'This is an unusual movement order?' I was told. 'Is it RAF or Army sponsored?'

'Er ... I'll be with the Army, I think.'

Such vagueness suggested an administrative minefield they would rather not enter. They saw that I was already permanently detached from my parent unit and was now to be detached from that detachment. Furthermore, if I was to proceed to Libya, as warned by the battalion, I would be detached from a detachment from a detachment – involving four time zones too!

Eventually, after much argument and anxious clock-watching, I played the only card I had.

'Look,' I pleaded. 'It's all a mystery to me, but my boss has told them I'm coming. How about giving me a seat as a birthday present? I'm 29 today.' I waved my passport again. 'It's all in there.'

Some years later, I volunteered to attend a survival course and, on arrival for instruction, was puzzled to be interviewed separately by the unit CO. Because my rank was 'higher than usual for trainees' – and was the same as his – he seemed certain that I had come to upend a long-standing and jealously-guarded succession policy. My assertion that I was innocently taking up a place allocated to my home station did not convince him and thus, apparently for political reasons, I became a marked man.

The second week of the course was held on a December Dartmoor, where we had little food, rest or shelter. Earlier we had learned how to make a tepee from a parachute, how to avoid capture by the 'enemy' and how possibly to supplement our meagre emergency rations. In this latter we were forbidden to approach sheep, so had to content ourselves with extracting small trout from the river.

A warm and well-fed film team came each day to turn our wretchedness into recruiting posters. We enviously scorned their comfort, but raided their helicopter for anything edible. The pilot's guard was distracted while two or three of us swarmed aboard, stole anything useful and then stuffed our pockets and mouths with the loose sugar found in their tea kitty.

After a day of hiding from the enemy, falling into flooded peat holes and reviewing our continued service in *this man's bloody air force*, our group was crouched miserably around a damp fire, sipping tepid nettle soup, when our instructional staff tormentors unexpectedly returned.

Again, I appeared to be the marked man.

'We've been reading your personal file,' they sniggered, handing over a small package.

Wrapped in yesterday's newspaper – itself a handy bit of kit – was an undersized sample of Mr Kipling's Exceedingly Fine Cakes, together with six small tins of beer; tantalising tastes each for the twelve of us.

'Happy Birthday!' the staff intoned, and melted into the night as my starving new friends gathered closely.

On the threshold of my service dotage, I again heard the claim that only in Southern California's balmy blue skies could proper conditions be found for high-altitude parachute training.

'Honestly, boss,' the lucky participants would protest, some of whom had returned many times. 'We only go to escape the British winter ... honestly.'

For my part, an unnecessary medical restriction and then increasing seniority had prevented earlier attendance, but eventually, and thanks to a sympathetic doctor – himself a parachutist – I joined the list to see for myself what all this California fuss was about.

From Day One, what could not be denied was that *out there* the skies were indeed blue to the very edge of space and progress was bewilderingly rapid.

Unfortunately, I suffered a recurrence of a chronic sinus complaint that became more obvious as we climbed higher into thinner air. It all climaxed on one sortie when I could not clear my ears and the aircraft made an emergency descent to deposit me, without ceremony – unused parachute and all – to await rescue on the runway.

'You the Brit that screwed the flight plan?' the American airfield team asked, and whisked me off to the unit's sick bay, which resembled a medium-size NHS facility. Here my *code in de node* declaration resulted in immediate grounding.

That might have been all right – I had accumulated a respectable jump total – but the exercise was drawing to a close and I was determined not to miss the final jumps.

For a couple of days I avoided the medics. Yes, I was grounded, and perhaps a British officer was not expected to break the rules, but they had not said for how long, so the game was on.

On the final day, two sorties were planned, and, safe in my grand rank, I declared myself fit for jumping that day. Bob, one of our expert cameramen, offered to fall with me, to get a souvenir shot or two on the way down, which would provide clear evidence to the sceptics at home that this increasingly 'desk-bound warrior' had indeed taken advantage of the clear blue skies.

We leapt out as a twosome at around 12,000 feet and, as my mentor swooped towards me, I struck a suitably heroic pose. He hung slightly above, so that the picture would include the odd square mile of California far below.

That's when our troubles began… I had an irresistible urge to clear my tubes while his hand-held shutter release failed, obliging him to reach up and operate his helmet-mounted camera directly. Accordingly, and because of our changing attitudes to the air stream – described as 120 mph in all the best books – we alternatively dived and soared past each other.

Clutching my nose, I swooped in a random fashion around the sky and, at each face-to-face encounter, grinned for posterity as Bob clicked manfully. Gravity, of course, worked throughout, exactly as advertised.

'Sorry about that,' I said after landing. 'My nose is clear now.'

'No problem,' Bob replied. 'I avoided a face full of boot. We'll see what comes out.'

Back in the UK, I received several shots of waving legs, the back of a helmeted head and one with a minute parachutist against a distant mountain.

'Never mind,' I consoled Bob, 'at least I got a couple of jumps on the last day – but only my flying log book will record what I did on my 46th birthday.'

Only in retirement did I regret not recording what exactly I had done on each other of my other 'Air Force Birthdays'.

7. IN THE LINE OF DUTY

Military people swear Oaths of Allegiance to Her Majesty and to do one's duty becomes a *sine qua non* for career survival.

Curiously, I have no recollection of doing that, but as I had been promising on my Boy Scout woggle since early teens to 'do my duty to God and my country', perhaps that vow had been carried over.

For the 'green' young officer at his first unit, however, what had been earnest airy-fairy discussion on the concept of duty as a moral obligation was unexpectedly expressed more bluntly.

'Here's the next job, laddie. Get on with it a.s.a.p.'

God, country or even Her Majesty were seldom invoked.

Just to fulfil primary duty was sometimes hard enough, despite expensive training, reinforced by wise counsel from superiors – usually in the form of terse rebukes.

Secondary duty was something else, and only the fortunate avoided involvement in this culture. A junior officer could be detailed to oversee any welfare activity –and with luck it might be within one's sphere of competence. To be Officer in Charge of a winning rugby football team was to gain a lustre that might burnish a young man's reputation. To be appointed 'in charge' of the station crèche, however, could be seen by some as a limitation to progress.

At one station I was 'volunteered' to the secondary duty of Secretary to the Officers' Mess Committee. This quickly converted me into a general dogsbody, accustomed to one-way conversations with senior mess members and loud complaints from all others, as I tried to explain policy that I barely understood myself.

Presidency of the committee was a secondary duty reserved for senior officers, who then became very visible to the Station Commander. No doubt because of this, my new 'secondary boss' tended to emphasise his instructions by identifying every task laid upon me as a *duty*.

'Your next duty,' he would say, 'Is to...' or, 'It is your duty to...'

On one occasion I was to arrange the off-stage accommodation of a showbusiness personality who had been hired as the star of a Mess cabaret. My further *duty*, the boss had instructed, was to meet, greet and generally look after our visitor. Naturally, the duty of hospitality would preclude my own relaxed preparation for the evening's show and so, yet again, my wife would have to collect the babysitter and then make her own way to the party.

That minor domestic upset was easily compensated for by the exciting prospect of being in close proximity to a household name, whose TV speciality was to take on a series of increasingly bizarre character roles. It promised to be a most agreeable duty.

Early that evening, after I had anxiously paced the floor, a lurid pink Rolls Royce pulled into the CO's parking slot outside the mess and the instantly-recognisable figure emerged. As apparently with all TV personalities – the word 'celebrity' was uncommon in those days – my man was smaller than I had expected and I relaxed a little. That is until I realised, with sudden dread, that he had adopted one of the many characters for which he was famous.

'Good evening,' I began formally. 'I'm the Mess Secretary. Welcome to...'

'Wizard!' he exclaimed, offering a palm-down hand, then gesturing towards his monstrous car. 'Nearly had a prang back there. Hun in the sun, what?' All this in high-pitched strangled tones, as heard in the best World War Two films.

'What time's take off, Wingco?' He continued, twirling a non-existent handlebar moustache.

'The cabaret begins at nine; we've a room and a meal for you.'

'Whacko!' he trilled. 'Bang on ... Know a little piece in town ... Twenty One Hundred you say? Roger, wilco. Return to base Twenty Hours.'

'Did the star get here okay?' the Mess President asked later in the bar.

'Er ... yes, he arrived early, but went off straight away.'

'What! ... Where?'

'Sir, I don't know.'

'Well, I suggest you track him down pronto. It's your *duty* to attend to the finer points of these events. He's costing enough.'

I passed another resigned thirty minutes in the mess foyer until our heroic guest returned. The CO's car now being in its proper place, the pink Roller was abandoned directly in front of the entrance, wheels-up on the lawn edge.

'Damn poor show,' he greeted drunkenly. 'Shum bounder shin my shlot.'

I escorted him carefully to back-of-stage, desperately hoping that he had merely taken on another character.

The main dining room had been converted into a 'night club' with tables around a central dance floor. A smooth conjuror followed by a near-naked woman singer got the cabaret off to a good start and – now that my guest knew where to go – I enjoyed a surreptitious ogle over my wife's shoulder, along with the best of them (after all, it was my *duty* to oversee the entertainment).

The girl concluded by inviting a not-too-unwilling medical officer to join her for a duet. In the front row the CO and his party were clearly uncomfortable with their close view of the anatomy on display.

'All in the name of medical science!' the Doc was heard to bellow happily.

I tried not to catch my president's eye.

At last, the big moment arrived and our expensive hiring made his entrance... Everybody was expecting a live presentation of his many well-loved TV characters – after all, I had met one earlier – so it was natural to assume that the inebriated buffoon we saw before us was one of those.

Introductory jokes at the expense of our seniors were hilariously received at the juniors' end but laughter became thinner when our men were ridiculed, then ceased altogether when our wives and girlfriends were abused. It was a relief when the act ended – in an arms-around-shoulders maudlin farewell with the singer and the conjurer – but my boss's gestures about *talks later* could not be mistaken.

The morning's 'wash-up' took a predictable path.

'Remind me how much we paid for last night's affair,' the President began.

'Three or four hundred, I fear, sir.'

'Indeed … Was the man drunk?'

'Perhaps he was playing one of his characters, sir.'

'The CO thinks he *was* drunk. You should have detected that and warned me. It was your *duty*. What were you thinking of?'

'I, er…'

'Well, I've got news for you. You're still mess secretary and your next duty is to work out some way of tapping mess funds for a new hat.

The CO's was found full of beer last night.'

8.   AIDE-de-CAMP? – ME?

Two photographs in my album – of the same occasion – evoke equal pride and embarrassment.

In the first, a battalion of troops marches past a senior officer of the Royal Air Force. At his side, sword to hand, parades an immaculate aide.

'That's me,' I tell my grandchildren.

The second picture shows an RAF flight lieutenant in a church. He wrestles uneasily with hymn sheet and sword.

Guess who?

The shots bring to mind a flight commander's career advice. 'You could never be an aide-de-camp,' he scoffed. 'Not tall enough, wrong accent and no 200-guinea uniform.'

I did have a trial run, however, and it began one bright Mediterranean morning as I admired the first rehearsals for a commemorative parade.

'Do you like ceremonial?' my company commander asked.

'Only as a spectator,' I replied.

'Well, you're not excused this time. Colonel Peter has invited the local RAF commander to review the parade and you will be the aide-de-camp.'

'But...'

'Quite so. I suggest you contact your RAF friends. The parade is a fortnight today.'

My list of 'buts' seemed endless. I had brought no formal uniform to this 'two-week' detachment, now into its third month; I did not own a sword; five years had passed since my last parade and, most worrying of all, what did an aide-de-camp actually *do*?

Luckily, it being Malta, it was no great distance from St Andrew's Barracks to RAF Luqa, but my journey there the following day – in an open-topped Land Rover – included passing through a slashing rainsquall.

A further complication was that my few pieces of recognisable RAF clothing – 'lost' in the local laundry – had been replaced by Army kit 'donated' from some mystery called the *Gee Ten Ninety Eight Store*. It was a comfortable rig that allowed me to fit-in easily, but I had an uneasy feeling that my light-blue colleagues would not take kindly to needle cords, bleached khaki shirt and, worst of all, red beret.

With brake-squealing panache, my driver delivered me to the RAF Headquarters, where I presented myself, black with rain, to an elderly squadron leader.

'Good morning, sir,' this with my best regimental salute, recently honed at the hands of my Company Sergeant Major. 'I am to be the Air Commodore's aide at next week's parade.'

The staff officer's astonishment went from angry demands for my ID to banishment to a far corner while he telephoned various minions.

'Is the Air Commodore reviewing a parade soon...? Did we know about an RAF officer living with that Army unit...?'

He had many other questions. Meanwhile, I watched my driver bailing out our jeep between immaculate salutes to all and sundry. At least one of us was keeping up the Regiment's good name.

I was saved by a clerk who brought news. Yes, they had heard there was an RAF officer at St Andrews and that was probably me. Yes, the Air Commodore had accepted the colonel's offer of a ceremonial aide when he reviewed the Rhine Crossing Parade. And yes, the real ADC was expecting a visit that morning.

'Extraordinary!' exclaimed the squadron leader. 'It seems I must believe your improbable tale. The office you want is last on the right... But never,' he wagged his finger angrily. 'Never appear improperly dressed again.'

Although the real ADC failed all the tests – not tall, probably wrong accent and an ordinary working uniform, she had everything in hand. She knew the timings, the parade format – more than I did at that stage – and had acquired a ceremonial sword for my use. Not in the least fazed by my damp clothing, she offered coffee and her book of words on sword drill. It was a timely lesson in what good aides actually do.

Clutching my weapon, I retrieved my driver – he appeared not to have eaten too many airmen – and returned, in bright sunshine, to barracks.

Still lacking formal uniform, I raided the recently-arrived heavy kit of my permanent successor. I would signal him tomorrow, but meanwhile we were of similar build, held the same rank and displayed the same badges. Good old black sticky tape could then reduce Peter's 32-inch inside leg to a more manageable 29 and a wad of rolled-up newspaper would make his cap fit. We even wore the same size shoes.

So I was ready – a brand-new ceremonial aide, eagerly reading the drill manual and threatening my batman with immediate banishment if he so much as sniffed *Brasso* at the sword's beautifully chased blade.

On parade day, everything began well. Pick-up at the Air Commodore's residence was to the second, it did not rain and plentiful Army salutes greeted our arrival, to fresh coffee, in a changing room in the mess.

I could get used to this ADC thing.

Following 'real' advice, I reminded the reviewing officer of the parade's salient points, then was surprised when he asked that I gave a surreptitious command to salute as we marched past the battalion colours during his inspection. This had not featured in the suggestions. Perhaps he too was a little uncertain about Army ceremonial.

The parade was superb, even my muttered 'hup' produced simultaneous salutes and, it might just be that the Army would graciously concede that the 'Crabs' were not too bad on the Square after all.

Then, as we climbed into the car for the church, I saw that my man's medal bar had unpinned itself and was about to part company altogether.

'That's just happened, I hope,' he said with a level stare.

'Indeed, sir,' I replied, fingers firmly crossed.' It caught your arm as you climbed in.

Oh yes, that's how ADCs earn trust.

The sweaty moments continued at the church door, where I saw an array of unclipped swords. Army scabbards hang in a short leather sheath, so it had been a matter of moments for my khaki comrades to disarm themselves before entering. We, however, carried our swords on slings – all in accordance with the book – and now faced a fumbled unclipping, followed by processing to the front, with braces dangling, so to speak.

As I dithered, the Colonel stepped forward in greeting and led the way inside, leaving me no choice but to follow immediately.

A real aide-de-camp, I mourned unhappily, would have unclipped everything in the car – and wasn't there something in the rules about weapons in church? In addition to those woes, I sensed a giving-way in the sticky-tape department at my ankles.

Naturally, my sword then got amongst my feet throughout the service and, at my every movement – to pray, to stand, to sit – clanked loudly on the stone floor. Two seats along, however, the Air Commodore appeared perfectly relaxed – no clanks whatever – but then, no sword either. Clearly, he had done this ceremonial thing many times before and I had completely missed his skilful disarming; too busy fretting about medals probably.

At the end of the service, as all officers formed up to 'stroll' to lunch, one or two of my comrades made polite enquiries.

'Is it an old Air Force custom, you know, never leave to your sword? … Can't have loose blades in the cockpit, after all.'

At the Mess, my Aide-de-Camp urbanity collapsed completely. Newsprint headlines adorned my damp forehead from the cap padding and Peter's trousers reverted to Dopey of the Seven Dwarfs length as the tape gave up the unequal struggle.

Having finally got the sword unclipped, but not the belt, I was forced to wander about with what looked like embroidered suspenders dangling below my tunic.

As the man had said years earlier. 'You'll never be an aide-de-camp: not tall enough, wrong accent and no 200-guinea uniform.'

9.   SHOWING THE FLAG

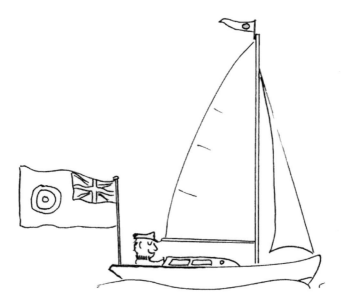

With equal degrees of pride and humility I supervised the yacht's departure as we left our home berth.

I was on board one of Her Majesty's training yachts, under the sky-blue RAF ensign, sailing as Deputy Skipper. My sailing experience, together with a formal qualification, had been deemed sufficient for that role and this was to be a 'check ride' by Jamie, the professional skipper.

As crew we had a bunch of youngsters, embarked for a week of character-building and big-yacht-handling. They came from the same station as me and I knew some of them well, but Jamie had announced that he would address me as 'Mister Mate'.

I had read the minutely detailed duties that came to the Mate – running a navigation plot, watch-keeping, sail changing – but none of these were too alarming; all well within the competence of an experienced hand.

'In addition,' Jamie then warned, 'I may impose certain other tasks as the need arises.'

That too brought no fears. I knew him by repute to be a calm and thoughtful leader, in the style of a diffident country gentleman. In any case, I had acquired considerable sea-time on these very yachts and so, anticipating a 24-hour or so crossing to the North Brittany coast of France, we sailed into robust Channel conditions ideally suited to our 55-foot vessel.

'The loo's not working,' one our female members reported as darkness fell.

'Ah,' said Jamie with a wise nod, 'it must be blocked.' And then to public acclaim, 'Clearing it is one of those extra tasks for Mister Mate that I mentioned.'

'By the way,' he murmured closely, with a conspiratorial wink over his shoulder. 'With ladies on board I have found it pays not to make too much of what caused the blockage, if you take my meaning.'

I soon found that *Every Mate's Yacht Repair Book* had little to say about how to unblock a through-hull flush toilet and so I spent an perplexing hour or so, head-down in a confusion of valves and noisome pipes, all of which seemed determined to roll out of reach as the boat galloped along.

Something doesn't quite match my status here, I thought, until, after almost complete dismantling, I found the cause and did indeed take Jamie's meaning.

In the morning we berthed alongside a massive granite quay at St Malo, with our deck a foot or two below the edge, thus offering intimate views of our lifestyle to the passing public.

'Mister Mate,' Jamie instructed, sounding like a latter-day Long John Silver, 'have the hands swab the decks and flake all the cordage. With that ensign up,' he nodded at our splendid azure bunting, 'we are technically one of Her Majesty's warships.' Let's show the flag properly.'

We were astern of a luxurious charter yacht that Jamie recognised as belonging to one of the big clearing banks and from which her crew admired our sleek, ocean-racing military purpose.

'Right, Mister Mate,' Jamie declared, well into his privately percolated real coffee. 'Go across and invite the skipper and his people on board. Let's give them a taste of Air Force hospitality. We might even get a return invitation. The girls will enjoy that. That boat's got showers and things.'

As I offered my invitation from the quayside, I took in superb teak decks, a spotless, tautly-spread sun awning and an abundance of what appeared to be soft, silken cushions. Of salt, blood, sweat and tears there was no sign, nor was there much evidence of character-forming either.

The five couples that teetered down our primitive boarding ladder wore what appeared to be spray-on pink slacks and striped Breton tops. However, their skipper, in accordance with his rank, sported immaculate whites, a brass-bound blazer and – Lord help us – a snappy, peaked yachting cap.

For our part, most had combed their hair and one or two even found clean jeans. Jamie, meanwhile, having rustled up copious supplies of wine and crisps, became the perfect host in his habitual gentlemanly manner.

Seemingly awe-struck, the visitors declared *what fun* it must be to sail on such a demanding racing machine, then one of the more gushing females wanted to see below decks.

'The Mate will show you,' Jamie commanded, so I led the way into our communal litter of damp sleeping bags, odd bits of interesting underwear and dripping condensation.

'Oh what *fun!*' the lady trilled. 'What *adventures* you must have in the RAF.'

Unfortunately, because I had failed to give notice of Jamie's intent to entertain visitors, our evening meal had been well under way as the party began and, lurking in the galley, was our cook-of-the-day. She was one of our stronger female personalities – it was, I swear entirely coincidental – and as we came down she was contemplating a large Dixie, full to overflowing with rapidly-solidifying Bubble and Squeak.

'Yes,' she muttered, with some venom, 'it is indeed such *fun!*'

We beat a hasty retreat to the cockpit and arrived just in time to watch Jamie, in a rare burst of extravagant gesticulation, anoint his opposite number's gleaming Chinos with a full glass of best *Supermarché* red.

'Steady on,' we cried, in a loyal attempt to lighten the disaster. That stuff's nearly two Euros a litre!'

'Quick!' our mortified leader cried. 'A cloth, a cloth!'

Clearly it was another Mate's special duty moment, so I ducked back under, brushed aside the mutinous cook and grabbed the nearest tea-cloth.

'Here...' I announced, demonstrating dazzlingly quick-reaction seamanship.

A greatly agitated Jamie seized this salvation and furiously mopped the affected parts.

As our visitor sat back in a small puddle of plonk, he watched in horror as Jamie's rubbing applied a dollop of congealed Bubble and Squeak to his most intimate area, where it made an interesting contrast to his newly-stained thighs.

The man rose and, now wearing the latest in grunge combats, gathered his appalled gang together and left abruptly.

A return invitation seemed unlikely.

'You know,' our cook declared into the silence, 'that was the high spot of an otherwise remarkably dull evening. Supper is ready ... *now*,' she continued ominously. 'It has been such *fun*.'

All eyes on our skipper, we waited fearfully for his lead. Not one of us moved.

'I think, Mister Mate,' he remarked pensively. 'We'll take down our special flag. We don't want to attract too much attention to ourselves.'

10. MY COLONEL WOULD LIKE A WORD, SIR

According to legend, a squad of armed recruits at a regimental depot were once ordered to '*Ground Arms!*'

By numbers, knees bending in unison, rifles were laid on the ground and, as the troops marched aside for foot drill, a grid of perfectly aligned Lee Enfields marked where they had last halted.

Seemingly – and it does appear unlikely – the drill corporal then dismissed the men, aside from their weapons, but in time for the next training session.

One recruit, in an anxiety of eagerness to be at that place first, forgot his rifle and raced ahead to be sitting at attention, bright-eyed and bushy-tailed, before his re-armed comrades tumbled in.

For the remainder of the day a solitary rifle lay at top dead centre of the parade square. It was still there as the squad was marched to their meal before the evening's 'bulling' boots and buffing up the floor.

At that establishment, it seems, the recruits kept their weapons with them in the barrack block, so our hero devised a simple plan. Using recently-learned infantry skills, he would creep through the shadows, pick up his missing musket and return unseen to base.

His approach went well and he reached the spot in a few bounds. Cradling the rifle in his arms, he straightened for his dash to anonymity.

'That man there! Stand still!' boomed out from the darkness. It was the Sergeant Major, who had watched and waited and who now marched on to instruct the lad in certain protocols.

Leaving the rifle was bad enough, but by far the greater sin was that of not picking it up by numbers, in the approved manner, and so being 'idle' on parade…

That story came painfully to mind during a tour of duty when my job was to train parachute instructors.

Officers and junior NCOs worked through the same syllabus of training over a four-month period. Because most of their customers-to-be would be from the Army – the RAF being responsible for parachute training of all British parachuting troops – it was entirely appropriate that the fledgling instructors should see where military life began for these people.

Many were of the Parachute Regiment and most others had passed, regardless of regiment or corps, through the Army selection system based at the Parachute Regiment Depot in Aldershot.

I had myself served with the small RAF unit permanently attached to the Airborne Forces and liked to think that I had absorbed some of the ethos of these troops. Why, I had even taken to the parade square myself when serving with a battalion overseas. Clearly, the Parachute Regiment Depot was the place to visit.

On arrival we were directed to park our minibus on the edge of the square. It was a surprising acceptance of the increasing need for car parking space, but at least purity was preserved by a not-to-be-denied painted boundary beyond which every vehicle was precisely aligned with its neighbour.

My party comprised four junior officers and four corporals all dressed, as was usual when visiting in those days, in 'best blues', brass buttons and all.

We were to disperse for lunch, so with a vague wave of the officers towards their mess on the other side of the square – 'I'll catch up, it's that way,' – I took the NCOs aside for a stern briefing.

'Now listen, chaps. You don't need to march as if on parade, but this is the regimental depot, so form up in pairs and keep in step, heads up …' In the corner of my eye, I saw the officers were moving away from the parking area '…and, above all, do not pass over this line onto the square. Got it?'

Four solemn nods and a collective twitching of ties.

'Okay, back here at …'

'Sir!' bellowed a distant but furious interruption. 'A word if you please!'

From the other side of the square, an immaculate military presence was approaching at quick-march pace.

'Right lads,' I said to the quaking corporals. 'Salute me now, about turn and scram.'

I had barely time to return their compliment when Nemesis was upon me.

It was the Regimental Sergeant Major, the senior warrant officer of the Parachute Regiment Depot and on his own patch – complete with red beret, royal coat of arms insignia, lightly starched shirtsleeve order and glittering pace-stick. To right and left, lesser beings – including a junior officer or two – dodged behind buildings and parked cars.

With some relief, I saw that my corporals had formed up smartly and were making proper military progress towards the mess hall, arms swinging and all.

Only as I turned towards the RSM did I get clear sight of my commissioned quartet.

But late, far too late.

The warrant officer swept past at about ten paces. With a quivering salute to me – straight out of Trooping the Colour – and a hoarse, 'Good morning, Sah!' he bore down on the slothful gang I had introduced to the sacred place.

In a loose huddle, caps at all angles, they had crossed the line and were cutting across towards the Officers' Mess.

And, dear God, one of them had a hand in his pocket and was slapping his gloves onto his thigh with the other.

It was upon him that the RSM descended, wheeling to a halt in a spurt of crushed gravel.

'Sir,' he menaced, 'I am saluting you.'

It was then that I saw that it was the miscreant's right hand – the saluting one – that was pocketed. Desperately, I hoped that he would not wave his left. Like the rifle in the story, that would only compound the crime of idle strolling on the Square.

I hurried forward, arms swinging, heels clicking, but could not save the lad.

The towering RSM leaned forward, distastefully, as if examining pond-life and, in a 'whisper' clearly heard by all present, including the drivers of passing traffic, delivered his coup de grace.

'You are an idle Royal Air Force officer, sir. My colonel would like a word with you.'

Then he turned to me.

'And you, sir,' with a contemptuous glance at my rank badges – equivalent to a captain. 'You should know better, sir. ... My colonel would like a word with you too.'

Clearly, I needed to review my syllabus concerning Army custom and usage. Oh... and possibly make no assumptions about officers' deportment.

11. SICK PARADE

In the ' Bad Old Days' a sick parade was just that: the ailing formed up at the unit sick bay and were marched into the medical officer in double time Similarly, *lying to attention on sickbed by numbers* was enshrined in the therapeutic drill book.

Matters had become a little less ritualised by my time, but it remained that the ailing reported *sick* on *sick parade*. None of this modern *appointment for consultation* jargon, if you please.

Happily, and thanks to a robust constitution, the majority of my contacts with medical officers were social in nature, even, on one occasion, sharing a double bed with the doctor during a 'sneaky-beaky' exercise in Bavaria after the accommodation plan went awry. He limited his morning report on my medical condition to a terse, 'At least you don't snore.'

Of course, there were the annual medical inspections to endure – one-sided conversations when continued fitness for employment was assessed. And there was the compulsion to remain fit that resulted from close contact with gangs of fit, macho young men, amongst whom only gaping wounds and imminent expiry would bring mutual sympathy for the sick.

So saying, at least one medic – himself a parachutist – was highly sceptical of such 'peer pressure'.

One time, after a couple of weeks of feeling 'not quite right', I finally succumbed and attended sick parade. There was nothing obviously amiss, but the doc took a blood sample – a first for me – 'so we can see if there's anything sinister going on.'

The significance of pathological analysis of a vital fluid passed me by – I was feeling better anyway – until three days later I was called by the sick bay.

'Your test results are back; you had better come across straight away.'

Such a summons – no waiting list – concentrated both mind and blood pressure and saw me parading at the double, to arrive at the doctor's in a mild sweat.

'Let me say what's *not* wrong with you,' he began, casually.

Hey, I thought, *this could be life or death here.*

He recited a list of conditions that would have defeated any spelling bee, all well beyond my comprehension, but apparently I was going to live.

'The real problem,' continued my saviour. 'Is that when you muscle mechanics get a sniffle ... that the ordinary bloke in the street wouldn't even notice ... you lot think you're dying. Now bugger off.'

It was the latest thinking in sympathetic care, right enough, but did ensure that I would dose my next fluey session with *Lemsip* and whisky in the good old-fashioned way.

Not long after that, however, there was a distinct 'click' in one ankle as I landed by parachute. It had not seemed a particularly 'hard' landing, but my usual spirited leap to my feet resulted in an agonised pitch forward. The drop-zone medical orderly brusquely set me 'aside' for collection later.

There were only two 'wounded' at the end of the programme: me, who could only hop and a concussed young soldier who could not see straight.

'The ambulance will drop you off at Casualty,' advised the medic. 'Keep your eye on the lad, he doesn't know what day it is.'

Twenty miles later we pulled up in a back lane beside the town centre hospital.

'I'm off shift now, boss,' the driver said. 'That's Casualty just up there, good luck.'

I suppose it was a parade of sorts; the soldier who could not see straight took half my weight and I steered. Gratefully, we flopped onto a row of seats and, grubby in our jumping overalls, soaked up curious stares from all around.

The real problem was that they had all checked in and we never did. After all, we were on sick parade and our last instruction had been to wait.

So we waited.

The seating bench next to us emptied and filled again.

We sweethearted cups of tea.

My companion had a little snooze.

Eventually, the system, in the form of an outraged senior nurse, took charge.

'Don't you people know *anything*?' she cried. 'Haven't you checked in yet?'

Matters speeded up then. The dizzy one was led away and I faced a harassed casualty doctor.

'That's a ruptured Achilles tendon for sure,' he declared, after my explanations.

'But I can...'

'Plaster room for you.'

'But I can flex my... an X-Ray perhaps?'

'Some sick parade this, mate,' said the porter, as he wheeled me along. 'I did nine years in the Mob ... not a scratch.'

Suddenly I had a gleaming white plastered leg, toe to crotch, and no arguing.

Back at base and admitted to Sick Bay for the night – *that plastering might cut off circulation* – the duty doctor was certain.

'That's not tendon rupture. What did the X-Ray show?'

It seemed the wrong time to confess an absence of hospital notes or X-Ray. It had been a long day, he was several ranks senior to me and lying to attention required concentration.

After a week, during which my wife endured bathing around a plastic-wrapped leg and a Highland Ball with peg-legged partner (she drew the line at my wearing the kilt) I was returned to the civilian hospital.

None of the military doctors had agreed on my injury.

Here, without further ado, my plaster was removed and, without X-Rays or extensive inspection, I was fitted with an elastic stocking.

At least the NHS sick parade was swift. I had learned the absolute requirement to check in on arrival.

At base again, a medical officer took a look.

'No X Rays? Well it's definitely not a ruptured Achilles. I reckon that's a deep muscle tear you've got there. You're one of these fitness freaks, so you should know what to do, but I'll put you to the physiotherapist anyway.'

Weeks later, and after countless daily sick parades, everything was coming good. The walking stick had been discarded, I was almost fully mobile again and about to be discharged as *fully repaired*.

'You know what, boss?' the physio said, as I endured a final session on his 'wobble board'. 'I reckon you've had a broken ankle all along and it's mended itself.'

Years later, during my pre-retirement medical examination, it seemed a good time to ask what my records showed.

'You know, Doc... parachuting injuries. Anything attributable to hazardous duty in the service of my country?'

'Nothing,' she said, after a cursory flip through. 'In fact, there's very little here about anything other than short-sightedness and perhaps mild insanity.'

So I was fit enough to return to the real world; no more sick parades; no more career-threatening medical inspections.

'However... I *have* noticed,' the doctor continued, taking hold of my head and twisting it beyond design limits. 'You've got restricted neck movement. Before signing you off, I'll refer you to a consultant. A final sick parade can do no harm.'

12. TICKS IN THE BOX

He could be Ace Of The Base, the finest leader since the Iron Duke and his CV might include high-grade training annotations of immediate relevance. At annual reporting time his boss might even comment favourably on the ambitious young officer's performance, but none of this would matter one jot if the record did not show success in the appropriate promotion exams.

To reach the stars, ticks in the box had to be acquired and local commanders were quick to remind their juniors that progress without them was impossible.

I don't recall ever being consulted about promotion as an ambition; it was simply demanded as a goal of all junior officers.

However, at my first unit I did mutter in half-hearted rebellion that after years of school exams, college 'finals' and, most recently, the Officer Cadet Unit, my exam days were over.

What heresy, simply not allowed, so not-so-subtle pressure was steadily applied until I felt obliged to apply for a place on the next promotion examination to flight lieutenant. It was, so the boss assured me, 'essential to clear each hurdle as soon as possible after achieving the rank below'.

Study had to take its place amidst the daily run of professional and domestic survival, so it did make sense – even I conceded – to get the required ticks early. After that, so the theory went, a reasonably 'clean nose' for the required time-in-rank would ensure eventual advancement.

In the Mid-1960s my exam comprised five papers over two days and I managed to crash one of them. Failure, I argued, was because of the 20-mile harum-scarum drive to the exam centre, but it might have been more to do with 'College Boy' complacency.

So I got a partial pass and endured the scorn of my squadron commander, whose dark hints passed from restrained to full on.

'Failure, even partial, is not an option, young man,' he threatened. 'Under my command ticks in boxes must be acquired.'

He was not too complimentary about my ace-of-the-base performance either.

What really hurt was that, a few years later, having taken the exam again and been promoted, that exam was abandoned by the RAF altogether.

However, by then I was being steered towards different, more senior ticks.

At the end of residential staff training – another ticked box – my tutor reminded me that as promotion to senior rank was hard won in my small branch, it was advisable to take the promotion exam as soon as possible.

'Promotion might be slow,' he warned, sounding like a well-worn recording, 'but impossible without exam success.'

So, in due course, I presented myself to a centre, where the President of the Examination Board took immediate exception to my casual dress.

In those days 'casual' for a serving officer with career pretensions meant tweed jacket, cavalry twills, regimental tie and gleaming brogues (no longer the homburg hat, thank goodness). My mistake had been to report directly off study-leave, thereby failing to acknowledge that promotion exams were a duty for which appropriate uniform was required.

The President – sternly and publicly censorious – was minded to deny me access to the examination, except that I was not under command. By being a visiting candidate from a small HQ just up the road, he knew that I answered to a commander of rank beyond the dreams of either of us. Based in a country manor house, it was known as a fairly 'laid-back' sort of place, so perhaps my mufti was interpreted as 'normal' for officers from there.

I took my place under the thoughtful, possibly envious, gaze of the other candidates and desperately tried to steer my subdued wits away from Dress Regulations towards the matter in hand. Even so, the deputy invigilator had the last word.

'It doesn't matter very much anyway,' he sneered. 'I'm to tell you that your posting came through this morning, but I don't know where.'

After this relaxed introduction to the morning's intellectual rigour, it hardly seemed possible that I could pass the exam and get the tick. But I did and, not too many years later, to everybody's astonishment, I was actually promoted.

At last – no more exams!

Now that I had reached the lower levels of senior rank, a meteoric rise to Head of the Air Force – well, okay Head of my Branch – would only be a matter of consistent performance in post, not offending too many senior officers and serving a few more years.

Of course, it was never that simple. New boxes to tick appeared instantly; a two-year correspondence course had to be completed. I had been half-way to promotion, but eventually a very average graduation ensured that my name was unlikely to appear on any imminent selection panel for Staff College. Therefore, the closest I came to RAF academe, that vital next stage for progress onwards and upwards, was when an old friend, in his early weeks as a student, invited me to attend a 'Bavarian Night'.

'It'll be great,' he enthused, as we spent an entire afternoon dreaming up suitable fancy dress for the occasion. 'Leather and frills is rig of the day.'

Tweed climbing breeches with thick sea-boot stockings were converted into *lederhosen*. White cargo-tape with felt-tip decoration was stapled into cross-chest braces. The girls found swirling dirndl skirts; we could have auditioned for *Sound of Music* with ease.

Our arrival at the college mess coincided with a quiet spell in the foyer, so Jerry and I rehearsed our knee-slap clog dancing while our wives took to the powder room.

A foursome in impeccable eveningwear strolled past.

'*Gute Nacht!*' we chorused, inaccurately, to their glares.

Jerry had recognised one of his tutors – 'Things can be a bit career-minded-stuffy here' – and we were still chuckling when the ashen-faced girls rushed out.

'Everybody in there is wearing evening dress.' Jerry's wife cried. 'They thought we were part of the entertainment troupe.'

'And not supposed to be in there with them.' My wife added.

Then two high-flying officers – fellow students of Jerry – came along. I knew them well from my own specialisation.

'Steady on,' they mocked, urbane in their dinner jackets. 'Nobody said Staff College entertainment would be such low quality.'

It was too late for retreat, but we did attract a special at-the-table tribute from the bare-kneed oompah band, and were joined by an American party – authentically kitted – who were delighted to see that some Brits could unbend.

'It said *Bavarian Evening*,' Jerry insisted. 'I must have missed where it said *national dress optional*.'

'This might cost you a few ticks on your way to stardom,' I joked. 'What do you think?'

'I'll just have to blame you if I don't make it.'

Jerry got his Staff College tick and I never returned.

Neither of us reached the very top, but otherwise did well enough. I like to think we got ticks that night for panache rather than erudite debate of strategic air power.

That's my excuse, anyway.

13. ENTENTE CORDIALE

Organising a sporting weekend at a military unit is fraught enough with home-grown booby traps, but when the visitors are from another country the occasion can become a whole new minefield.

We were to entertain staff and cadets from the French École de l'Air. Rugby and fencing were the chosen sports, but legend had it that the French would be more concerned about social aspects than with match results.

Thankfully, only the games were my responsibility but, as often was the case, the disproportionate worry was the Pandora's Box of minor protocol issues.

'You're a college boy,' my warrant officer remarked mischievously, with a week to go. 'What's the French national anthem?'

From deep within my schoolboy data bank came the immediate answer, *Allons enfants de la Patrie* ... I don't know why, perhaps I had been a French patriot in a former life.

'No, not the words, sir, it's the *tune* we need.'

Backed by his grinning subordinates, he was brandishing our departmental long playing vinyl record of popular anthems.

'The record sleeve will tell you the track number. Just count from the edge ... it's simple.' These were days long before CDs and their helpful digital screens.

'Ah, but we've lost the sleeve and none of us knows the tune.'

And so another dim memory was dredged while they matched my hesitant whistle to the LP. On the record, however, the French followed the German anthem and the Warrant remembered a wrong track once being selected at a critical moment by a dim disc jockey who could not count.

'Fear not, boss,' he cried, 'I'll blank off all the other tracks with black tape. That way, if the duty idiot misses on the day, we'll just get a ruined stylus and not an international incident.'

Next day, one of the female corporals came in, holding the horizontally-striped Dutch flag against her chest, as if choosing a dress in a trendy boutique. 'Which way do the stripes go on the French flag?' she asked innocently. 'I thought it was vertical, but this doesn't look right.'

It sounded like a try on, but I could not be certain, so delivered a stern homily to the whole crew: the French Tricolour is vertical stripes, short side to pole, red end out. And make sure ours is the same size, or bigger. Flags matter here.'

This was received in amazed silence, but as I left, distinct Inspector Clouseau stage whispers came from the back row.

'Eff yew a leesance for thees fleg?'

I knew it; it *had* been an impudent wind-up all along.

Then it was confirmed that the French party would include NCOs, so my lot began training for a spell of serious and expensive bar athletics. The warrant officer thought fifty pounds – quite a sum in the mid-1970s – from my entertainment fund would be about right. I thought he meant for the weekend, and change to come; he meant the first evening.

On the day, we met the visitors at the airfield. Our commandant made a brief welcome, the cadets were marched onto buses and those of us hosting a French couple took them to our cars. Spoken English seemed at about the level of our French, so we were quickly into animated Franglais.

'Ah!' exclaimed Madame. 'We are at home already. We have such a car.'

Our recently-acquired Renault 16 was a nice touch, I thought, even if my wing commander thought it one hosting step too far. The ice was further broken when the French major and I collided at the driver's door: he having gone to the front passenger side and me to drive.

During the short journey to our house my new friend suddenly grabbed for the wheel as we closed with the first oncoming vehicle. The little tussle for control took us momentarily onto the grass edge and was followed by a burst of too-rapid-for-me French.

'My husband say sorry,' explained Madame. 'It is French car like we have, but he forget you drive on left side. It is first time in England.'

At home our two little daughters observed everything closely, the quicker to adopt the more dashing foreign ways. Saturday breakfast went especially well. They were introduced to croissants and strong coffee and particularly admired Monsieur's way of dunking his pastry into the drink.

Not too keen on coffee, perhaps, but croissant messily soaked in orange juice was perfect.

Afterwards, we passed the morning rambling around the local Saturday market, drinking more coffee with mutual practice of English and French.

I went into work well before the afternoon start time and was relieved to find a functioning electric piste, pristine protective clothing and a happy fencing master. At the rugby pavilion the referee had arrived and a magnificent French flag – not a Dutch one its side – fluttered proudly.

Best of all, my warrant officer assured me, thanks to Sellotape at all dangerous places, only the *Marseillaise* could possibly be played.

'There is one problem though,' he continued, just as I relaxed. 'How're you fixed for another sub? We had a lot of Anglo-French relations in our mess last night.'

'Just a minute, tonight's affair is in *our* mess for *everybody*.'

'Indeed, sir,' he replied, without a blush. 'But unfortunately the French have invited us to sundowners before we go to your place. It's their custom, you know.'

Shortly after midnight – few could recall the match results – I was astounded to see one of my NCOs urbanely leading the French general's wife around the empty dance floor, both chattering away, twenty to the dozen.

'Hey,' I said to the warrant officer. 'We know she has little English, but you never said he can speak French.'

'He can't, boss, but what a mover! When you can dance ballroom like that, who needs words?'

Our Monday morning debrief judged it a successful weekend with our visitors' only moderate sporting interest being overshadowed by their promise of even more and better socialising when we visited Salon the following year.

Alas it was not to be.

At the planning stage 'that lot' at Headquarters moved the goalposts and, to the amazement of the French, no aircraft seats were made available for our wives.

It was probably just as well. My children were still dunking everything. It must not become habitual.

14.   FIRING DETAIL ... KNEEL!

My wing commander was at his mischievous best.

'Right, King of the Oddballs,' he grinned, 'this job is right up your street. A real career enhancer.'

I sighed reflectively. The boss was certainly right about my 'kingdom', but some of the 'enhancing' had been hard to recognise.

Officially, I was responsible for the domestic affairs in the lives of around one thousand trainees at a large technical training unit. Bed space inspections, foot drill, pay parades – after a near-vertical learning curve – had all become my daily bread and butter. It had been the additional duties – the oddballs – that had, like the old Chinese curse, led me into 'interesting times'.

These had ranged from supervising the welfare of a baby donkey, newly-acquired as the station mascot, to acting as mentor to a newly-commissioned officer. This latter fell well within my expertise, except that she was a leggy blonde, not much older than my teenage daughters. Her modern interpretation of the expected courtesies from juniors to seniors included rushing up to me in the mess bar with happy cries of 'Sugar Daddy!' It may have been flattering to an ageing, still red-blooded male, but in the eyes of the more conservative, it hardly bettered my career.

Although my superior expressed much sympathy throughout all this, and we frequently cried on each other's shoulders over an evening whisky, he took care to remind me that he had a large training school to run, so such mysterious problems were mine to solve.

'The good news,' my boss continued, pouring more coffee, 'is you'll personally get to meet the Chief of the Air Staff. That's got to be good for any career officer.'

'Er... that depends on how we meet,' I countered, suspiciously.

'As you know, CAS (he used the common acronym for the RAF's top man) is visiting the school in a couple of weeks. Well...'

'You don't mean I've got to act as doorman?' I interrupted. After a year in my catchall sort of job, anything could happen.

'No,' the boss was enjoying this.

'Not the bloody donkey!'

'Not even that.'

He then explained that our Station Commander had suggested that to see other, non-technical work on the station, the Air Chief Marshal could do the mandatory range firing that all officers had to complete.

'That's your empire,' the wing commander reminded me. 'Not only will you get to meet our supreme leader, but you'll be training him too.'

It was more unknown territory and the expert, my junior RAF Regiment officer, was on leave.

First call, then, was to his flight sergeant.

He was man of relentless professionalism, renowned for his daily run with a brick-filled rucksack. His eyes had lit up when we first met. 'At last! The Airborne Brotherhood,' he had declared, gesturing at our mutual parachute badges. 'Too many technicals here for simple soldiers.'

'Morning, Flight Sergeant.' The full title was proper. After all, I was about to issue him formal instructions involving no lesser person that the Chief of the Air Staff. Normally, because of an elaborate Polish family name, he was universally known as *Flightski*. 'The Chief of the Air Staff... yes, the real one... wants to do his annual shoot when he visits here next week.'

Flightski sipped his coffee warily.

'Can you organise that, please?'

Not a blink.

'Okay, Boss, no problem.' He set his mug carefully on the floor. 'Only one thing... You know, man-to-man, like... Don't get me wrong... But is this a *real* shoot, or just going through the motions? You know... pushing pencils through the target bullseye?'

Such a fraud had never occurred to me – another part of the vertical learning curve – another oddball?

'A proper shoot, Flightski. Real bullets, honest scores and, above all, *you* in charge.'

'Got it, Boss.' He stood to leave. 'Wonder when the Chief last fired a pistol?'

I took my plan to the Wing Commander.

'Sounds good,' he said. 'You can't fiddle the scores, that would be all wrong and the Great Man must see that we do things properly here. Anyway, over to you, sport. Like I've always said, I'm radar. All this jock-strapping guns stuff is your baby. Okay for a beer tonight?'

My career moment drew near and I waited at the small-arms range to greet the Chief of the Air Staff, my station commander and my wing commander; even the personal aide was senior to me. Dress for the day was best blue uniform, but at ease beside me, Flight Sergeant Ski presented a magnificent recruiting poster image of a fighting soldier. Pressed combats, gleaming calf-length boots and full belt order. On a table lay a selection of lightly-oiled 9mm Browning pistols.

The Station Commander seemed a little anxious, but a series of surreptitious winks and a thumbs-up from my immediate boss said all was well.

Flightski immediately entered the as-per-the-book procedure necessary when handling loaded firearms. He had suggested that to preface his commands with 'Chief of Air Staff...' would be too much of a mouthful, 'Detail...' would be crisper, punchier.

I had agreed, but had omitted to seek the Station Commander's sanction of this near-sacrilege. Consequently there was a deal of nervous blinking when Ski, indicating the table to CAS, and in tones normally used towards raw recruits, bellowed.

'Detail... with a magazine of nine rounds... Load!'

The eminent student obeyed every sharp command without hesitation and the plywood target was peppered from the conventional standing position. Even the CO – he was a radar man too – began to relax.

A fresh target was set up. The pistols were reloaded. Flight Sergeant Ski moved forward a pace or two.

'Firing detail...' he warned. 'Kneel!'

With a noticeable squelch, the most senior knee in the entire air force rocked forward onto the foam rubber mat that, unknown to us all, had soaked up much of the puddle it covered.

It was the one unchecked item on my list, but as my immediate superiors turned away from my doomed career, Ski's next command boomed out.

'Detail … at the target in front … in bursts of two rounds … Fire!'

Between bangs, I flipped desperately through my mental training manual. Please God, let firing from the prone position not be next in the drill.

Thankfully it was not, and as Ski noted his pupil's genuine accuracy at the targets, and we all studiously looked anywhere but at the previously immaculate barathea, the aide took me aside.

This is it, I quailed, career in ruins again, and what does an Air Chief Marshal's uniform cost to dry-clean?

'Well done,' he said. 'An unusual item for a visit. CAS enjoyed it too, you've got a good man there.'

Later, in the bar, my boss quipped that not many officers could claim that the Chief of Air Staff had saved their career. The CO had offered anxious apologies for the wet knee, but CAS had made nothing of it and heads were not to roll.

A week later, I had the official photos. It might have been a processing error, but there seemed to be undue focus on a certain right knee. Also, and again I could not be sure, the CO wore a decidedly out-of-his-depth expression.

'I suppose we could do some airbrushing on the negatives,' mused my wing commander.

'Steady on,' I cried. 'That's a bit technical. Well outside my remit!'

15. IT WAS A MAN'S WORLD

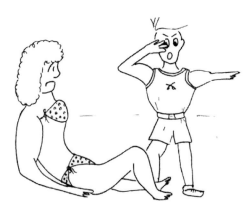

Arguably, any male officer of my generation will be uneasy at the sight of armed women, where the presence of the awkward sword or rifle seems all wrong somehow.

Our only defence can only be that we are products of our times and that these latter have changed.

As for me, having had no brothers, sons, nephews or, eventually, grandsons, how could I possibly be a male chauvinist? I had even been subordinate to a female commanding officer. A fine and sympathetic leader, her exceptionality arose from an eminence won in competition with men.

Even so, it was not until the mid-1970s that even I re-marked that females were becoming increasingly visible in what had always been a robustly masculine world. I was serving at a large, multi-function training unit that was very much a Royal Air Force showpiece. This status gave our daily affairs an urgent political self-consciousness that afforded those of my naivety ample opportunity to exercise *Mouths, Foot Putting Into, Officers For The Use Of.*

My responsibilities included fitness and sports training for trainee officers, all recent graduates of the university system and mostly male. To do this we enjoyed unrivalled sporting facilities and I was required to manage what, at that time, was possibly the biggest leisure centre in the county. Surrounded by manicured lawns, immaculate cricket wickets, a full-size swimming pool and a devoted grounds staff, it was Arcadia for a young officer of my profession.

And so it was, but for the aforementioned politics.

One warm summer's morning my staff were seriously distracted from their stern military duty by a group of nubile, bikini-clad women sunning themselves on the grass outside our main entrance.

'Now there's a sight for sore eyes,' the warrant officer declared wistfully. 'Makes you wish you were young again.'

Privately, I probably agreed, but in this instance things had gone just too far. Delightful though the scene was, I had a military training facility to run here and self-righteously went out to say so. Duty can be a hard taskmaster.

They could not be female cadets – there was not that number at the whole unit – so they must be a visiting group from the local swimming club that used our pool under formal licence. Unfortunately, my military authority was diluted because I was still wearing teaching whites – not a rank badge in sight – so meaningful intervention would have to rely on personality alone.

'Ladies,' I announced, desperately trying to maintain eye contact above the very brief costume, and uncomfortably aware of the grinning faces in the staff-room window. 'We cannot have this.' In the middle-distance I saw our next cadets' class approaching, marching in column of route, arms swinging, eyes to the front … all male. 'This is a military training establishment, not some sort of layabout's lido. If you are going to sprawl about the place, have the decency to cover yourselves. Better still, hide yourselves behind the building.'

The pompous little speech had an immediate effect and, as the cadets came to a heel-stamping halt at the gymnasium, the women gathered their scattered clothes and grumbled off the scene.

At the end of that week I was unexpectedly summoned to attend upon my divisional commander. During a largely one-sided conversation he listed my usual long-standing transgressions: cricket score box not yet painted; horses still crossing the rugby pitch; too much chlorine in the swimming pool... Naturally, despite these being quite out of my control, I promised immediate attention to each.

'Oh, and by the way,' he concluded. 'My wife …'

His ringing phone left me in a fever of horror. Surely his wife had not been amongst the anonymous Yummy Mummies? She knew me well and would have recognised me at once. Please say it cannot be so.

'Right,' the Great Man resumed. 'My wife needs more support in the Wives' Club. I have better things to think about than this, but as a start, ask your flight lieutenant whether his wife is with us or against us at this place.'

Things certainly were changing, I reflected, if Air Commodores had to include such matters when giving instructions.

Next call that morning was on my wing commander, to give a summary of activity. Relaxed in his appointment, he normally gathered his section commanders – often over lunch – to close the week with brief notes on achievements and problems. On this occasion, however, he had asked me to attend earlier 'for a private chat'.

'Ah, yes,' he said to my salute. 'Do come in. Er ... what a lovely morning... Look,' he appealed uneasily, 'I'd prefer not to get involved in this. We've all got more important things to do, but times are changing...'

This was a man I barely recognised, not at all the usual confident leader.

'Fact is, old boy, there's been a complaint that a group of wives were insulted by one of your staff at the swimming pool; something to do with revealing too much. Can I leave it to you to sort out?'

Although most of my subsequent service continued in the comforting, mostly male environment of old, history will doubtless show that female emancipation accelerated – there was no sound reason for it not to – until the Air Force employed female pilots and a separate women's service no longer existed.

And so retirement came and I took to attending reunions. My veterans' club allowed only male membership. After all, the military specialisation had been men-only since its beginnings in 1940. However, times had been a-changing and by the mid 1990s there were fully-qualified and 'badged' women in the ranks.

We old duffers eventually got around to discussing how this phenomenon would affect us. A firmly applied rule had always been that women could never attend our annual dinner, but a recent amendment graciously allowed them to escort the more infirm to the venue's door. At the AGM an anguished circular argument raged. Tactfully, perhaps, no women were present.

'Women are now eligible to serve in the specialisation and therefore can join the club.'

'But it's a men-only organisation.'

'Ah... but times have changed. There are even now two fully qualified women.'

'We'll have to take a vote.'

'No need. They are qualified and fall inside the rules.'

'But they're women ...'

The retired senior officers kept silent. We were no longer in command – or even influential – and certainly were not male chauvinists, were we? Eventually the vote was taken and properly recorded in accordance with the constitution. The girls were in.

Times indeed were a-changing.

The evening began with pre-dinner drinks in the bar and on this occasion a tight scrum of retired warrant officers and senior NCOs took up one corner. Officers were most definitely excluded.

'They're up to something,' I remarked to my old CO, now a brother veteran. 'Just like the old days.'

'Perhaps they're angry at this afternoon's vote,' he laughed.

'No they're not, look.'

The crowd had parted momentarily to reveal the centre of attention. Dressed in a glittering mini-dress, gym-toned legs to the armpits, was our newly-elected member.

The blazered backs of the one-time anti-women brigade closed ranks again, hiding her from officers' view.

'Oh well,' we said, happy that we were not the only dino-saurs, 'it's good to see that some things never change.'

16. POLITICAL CORRECTNESS

Junior officers and gentlemen, we were often instructed, should conduct their lives in respectful awe of the dignity of women, religion and politics.

Required behaviour in these matters was earnestly recommended by the Little Blue Book and sternly imposed by our betters. Loose gossip concerning women was forbidden, but, we would ask, was it OK to *speculate* about loose women? Regardless of faith, church parades were sometimes compulsory, but could we argue theology in the bar? To avoid the third prohibition, however, it was safer just to remind ourselves that our boss was HM the Queen and leave political manoeuvring to others.

It was not known as Political Correctness in those days, but that is what it was, and it made for a certain naivety in the face of the professionals; an innocence that sustained me throughout my service – almost.

Early in one tour of duty, the mystifying entry *Chain Gang Day* appeared on my inherited wall planner. Apparently this was the station's annual reception of all the mayors and senior councillors from the surrounding towns. They would form a sizeable party in which chains of office, chauffeured limousines and statements of influence would vie for attention. I was 'volunteered' to the conducting team.

A long afternoon would begin with a tour of the station – including an opportunity to fly in one of our gliders – and end with an early evening reception.

All began smoothly – admire a mayoral chain then step back to receive a potted history of the borough in question. This, in turn, would provoke a competing version from another, usually of different political colour, until we, as hosts, quickly became superfluous.

This continued to the airfield, and I thought things were going quite well until the senior pilot came across.

'We'll have to abandon the final launch,' he announced from behind his hand.

'Oh … running out of time?'

'It might be politically sensitive.' He gestured covertly towards a broad lady towering over a slim glider. 'Believe me, there's no way she will fit into that.'

'God, I hope you haven't actually taken a tape measure to her.'

The choices were to declare operational problems or rustle up one of the roomier powered machines sometimes used to tow the gliders aloft.

We settled for guile – after all, our guests were politicians – and the launch crew manufactured an esoteric winch failure

– would you believe it? Fortunately, the lady confessed that she had been uneasy about the lack of engine on the sailplane anyway, so honour, political face and our programme were saved in equal measure.

For the evening reception the plan was for each officer, accompanied by his wife, to 'close-host' a guest couple through a well-honed ritual: introduction to the station executives, then circulate with, at all times, fully topped-up glasses. The Little Blue Book, of course, advised a strictly neutral political stance.

A further requirement was to await the subtle signal that warned of the drinks drying-up. This would prompt the gracious hosts to round-off the chit-chat and ease the visitors towards the door and their waiting municipal carriages.

Then we would all heave a sigh of relief, rush home to change out of uniform and return an hour later for a private party, to include a fish-and-chips banquet delivered in bulk from the local chippy.

So, after the excitements of the afternoon, my wife and I duly 'collected' our assigned guest on arrival. He wore a magnificent golden collar and carried an ancient municipal title from our neighbouring city. We were fortunate to conclude the required courtesies with the station commander early, so we could relax and take the visitors around the company.

To our dismay, our conventional opening politeness – How long in their town? How long in office? – was quickly silenced by a rebuff of small-talk and a wish to inspect some of the other public rooms.

Luckily, we had a splendid grand entrance foyer, complete with a sweeping staircase and laid-up squadron colours. This had always been a perfect 'ice-breaker', but while I was explaining the tradition of flags, the man announced his distaste for 'the military', the 'officer class' and, 'what's more, the taxpayer paying for this sort of junket.'

The Little Blue Book – as so often in real life – left us floundering in procedural deep water, duty-bound to offer unstinting hospitality but forbidden to say that, actually, it would be paid for by a collective charge on us all.

When we returned to the main group, my immediate boss took me aside.

'Missed you there for a while,' he murmured. 'Problems?'

'No, we will survive... but you owe me a drink.'

'I know,' the Wing Commander continued *sotto vocco*. 'The Sheriff is well known for his extreme views. Nothing personal, it's just your turn. Good luck.'

Our guest knew that a riotous party was sure to follow and began to show distinct signs of staying on, invitation or not. My wife and I were answering his unsubtle hints with vague, 'We're-not-sure... babysitters, you know...' waffle when the *drinks-tap-off* signal was given and the crowd began to thin.

Our man set about lighting his pipe yet again – these were days when hospitality demanded tolerance of that – and, as I had noticed, returned his dead match to the box. As always, ignition required several attempts.

Suddenly, with only three groups remaining, there was a sharp *Whoosh*, a mini-mushroom cloud and we were alone in the middle of the big carpet.

'If that was a bomb,' I said, with a suavity that would have graced any etiquette book, 'the military police may have a few questions.'

Spluttering about burning matches in full boxes, but being sorry to miss the party, our guest nearly ran to his car.

Now to convince my boss of my innocence...

'That was a neat trick,' he said. 'I approve. However did you get it into his pocket? Must remember that for next time.'

The following week we were required to register on the local Electoral Roll.

'I think we might have blown it,' was my wife's only comment.

17. IT'S AN INDULGENCE

The theory was impeccable. You completed an application form – bright yellow paper – begged a sponsoring counter-signature from your boss, paid a nominal sum, then eagerly anticipated an aircraft seat allocation. Dependents could be included – and the whole world was your oyster. Known as *Indulgence Flying*, was it the ancestor of budget, no-frills?

There were, however a few snags. Flight, date or even destinations were not guaranteed and seat allocation was not confirmed until very late – sometimes at the check-in desk – and could be denied even then. Oh … and you could be off-loaded at an intermediate stop in favour of a higher-priority passenger.

My first direct contact with Indulgence Flying was during a flight to an airfield in Libya, not far from Tobruk. I found myself beside a young woman travelling alone. I was on a duty ticket and enjoying the rare treat of flying in a passenger aircraft, a huge improvement on having to squeeze in beside piles of netted freight.

The woman told me that her husband was at a Naval HQ in the Gulf – they had been apart for months – and that she would join him for some local leave. Wasn't this Indulgence business wonderful?

That all changed at RAF El Adem, my destination in Libya and a woeful place, even for duty passengers. Luckily, I would remain there only long enough to sign for a Land Rover before disappearing into the vast desert training area.

Equally luckily, for my own conscience, I had not described to the woman how awful a spot I thought El Adem to be. This was as well, because she and her luggage were 'off-loaded' there in accordance with the seat allocation pecking order. I learned later that she would be required to make her own accommodation and feeding arrangements while hanging about to get on a later flight.

No doubt the young woman was not completely ignored by the staff at El Adem and, equally without doubt, she did reach her destination eventually, but she lived in my mind's eye thereafter, tearfully alone in a dusty concourse and at the mercy of events.

There were too many residual uncertainties in the Indulgence process for my taste, and I never came to trust it. So saying, it was inevitable that there came a time when it would have been foolish not to take advantage.

By now promoted to senior rank and appointed to a large HQ, I was to visit Gibraltar as part of my duties. By judicious calendar adjustment I was able to include a Bank Holiday and my colleague on the Rock was more than happy for my wife to go out and be accommodated with me. It would be the first time, she reminded me with feeling, that she would get something back for her years of following the flag.

On the day, and because of the abiding El Adem memory, together with legendary versions on the same theme, I was reluctant to release our road transport from the departure airfield until my wife had been checked in and a valid boarding card issued.

I was then puzzled to be declared 'Officer i/c Troops' for the flight. 'You're the senior officer on this passenger list, sir.'

The mystery was compounded by a sketchy explanation of my duties: looking after the passengers if we landed somewhere other than our intended destination, and maintaining in-flight discipline. Was this not the crew's responsibility? Still, it was a civil airline on military contract, so I took it to be another unfamiliar feature of Indulgence, and still not entirely trusted.

Happily, as Officer i/c I was required to take the forward row of three seats to myself, so my wife and I did indeed indulge ourselves with elbow and legroom while everybody further back behaved themselves, and the captain managed to find Gibraltar first go.

After that, my duty visit, followed by suitable social activity, was a delight.

Indulgence rules had it that return passage could only be confirmed close to the departure date. It was also important to ensure that the departure field had received a separate application.

So, as our departure was planned for the Tuesday, it seemed prudent to get my wife's word to the appropriate ear in person, even though it was Bank Holiday Monday.

At the Air Movements desk, my query produced much muttering and paper shuffling, but no straight answers on anything. I began to doubt my own 'duty' seat until the clerk advised that I would be returning as 'Officer i/c' again.

'Ah,' I cried with relief, 'that means at least two seats for me alone ... Yes?' More head-down consultation of lists followed, but these were, they claimed, incomplete, so the Indulgence allocation could not be made until just before departure.

I was poorly placed to argue; the unit had already been most generous. I was unsure of the Indulgence rules but, most importantly, I did not trust the system; in my mind I saw that abject woman at El Adem again.

'Forget it!' I snapped. We were running out of time, so I rushed to the British Airways office to buy a 'walk-on' single journey ticket for the morning flight. To hell with the cost, my wife was not going to be abandoned on the Rock to await the next military schedule – possibly in three days – while I took my duty seat home.

Unfortunately, she would arrive at Heathrow while the 'trooping' flight, two hours later, would set me down at Luton. Worse, my driver and empty car would meet me there, while she would have to organise her own onward transport.

My little cache of domestic 'Good Boy Brownie Points', accumulated by including her on my visit, was diluting to nothing by the minute.

I saw her off and reported as Officer i/c Troops to the next-door desk – being Gibraltar, everything was on the same site. The RAF Movements staffs were no more forthcoming about my potential duties than previously, but there were empty seats a-plenty. However, and much to my fury, I was required to sit in lonely eminence in a row of three and was not at all impressed to be advised by the steward that even if the cabin had been fully occupied, those seats would have remained for my use alone.

Remonstration would have been pointless. My wife was now well on her way, albeit with a resigned sigh, and again my cabin crew were employees of a civil airline on contract to the military. They probably had less understanding of the Indulgence system than me.

I met my wife again when my car passed her as she began the mile or so walk from the nearest bus stop to our house. At least I had carried the luggage, but I was not going to be caught again.

'You're a married man,' I reminded the driver, as my wife boarded in menacing silence. 'This is now a survival exercise, rules or no rules.'

A week or so later – still wondering whether I was forgiven – our elder teenage daughter confessed that she had thrown an unauthorised house party during our absence. There had been some collateral damage, which had puzzled my wife, although I had noticed nothing.

The final 'go' for the shindig, however, had not been given until we had confirmed that my wife was definitely on the outbound flight, thus demonstrating that the girl had a better grasp of Indulgence flying matters than me.

That the same daughter announced, some years later, that she was going to marry in Hong Kong – thus obliging me to negotiate the whole Indulgence minefield once again – is, of course, an entirely different story.

18. LOOPING THE LOOP

Keeping in touch with old friends within one's RAF specialisation was relatively straightforward and I was helped in this by returning to the same unit in four separate appointments.

However, matters were naturally less intimate in the wider Service, even when the entire RAF came to be an average 'gate' for Wembley Stadium.

Gordon and I shared the same class throughout school – except that in the Sixth Form he took Sciences and I Arts. Then, with fond farewells, we entered the big wide world of college life; he to Birmingham, me to Durham, and I would never see him again, or so it appeared.

I had heard that Gordon was an RAF maritime patrol pilot, so, for the next 16 years, every time I met somebody from that world, the question would be the same.

'Have you ever come across my old school chum Gordon…?'

And the answer was always the same. No.

Apparently Gordon rarely carried a parachute; I would not fly without one. Different air force, you see.

In the mid 1960s our immediate neighbours in married quarters were transport pilots and Mike's little daughter became fast friends with our tot – we still have a photo of 'potty training' underway in the garden.

Doug, our other pilot neighbour of those days, had no children, so my wife, struggling with the third nappy of the morning, would enviously watch his elegant young wife jump into her MG sports car and whirl away to glamorous employment in town.

It was wonderful company, but at the end of the tour we all moved on with the traditional farewell, 'See you 'round.'

In fact, my wife and I maintained contact with Mike and family – even serving together again at another station – but Doug would be lost to us, or so it appeared.

During my next tour I was attached to an Army battalion that regularly sent me into Libya. In theory, my task was simple: set up a drop zone, receive paratroops from an aircraft, count heads and then go home with the soldiery. Then, a week later, I would be off to Libya again – Cyprus on a good day – and do it all again.

One such trip accumulated problems from my arrival. There was no accommodation for my batman/driver, I was warned, and only threats of putting him up in 'Officers' Country' got my man food and shelter.

Then I learned that my aircraft had failed to leave the UK, but on the promise of an amended schedule the colonel had decided to go ahead with the exercise and that I was to 'sit things out' until further instruction. The message came second hand, and included four alternative plans over three time zones. The Operations staff did their best, but were having difficulty accepting a lone RAF officer wearing a Red

Beret and followed everywhere by a fully-armed Parachute Regiment soldier.

I sent him off to acquire a Land Rover. At least then we could go for a look-see – but that meant I had to attend a briefing on World War Two minefields that might exist in my chosen piece of desert.

'The mines cover and uncover as the wind blows,' I was warned. 'They are marked by lines of stones.'

'Right,' I acknowledged, in suitably John Wayne tones, and peered at the map. 'How do we know which is the safe side?'

'You don't.'

My long-suffering servant went off to acquire some sand-bags for our vehicle's floor and to deposit our weaponry in the armoury.

That evening a transport aircraft came in from Cyprus and I wandered out to talk to the crew; it would be nice to recognise a sympathetic face.

'Hey,' the pilot shouted down from the flight deck. 'What are you doing here?' It was Doug. 'How long has it been? Come on up.'

'I'm with the Army at the moment, how far back do you want to go?'

'Christ, I always did think there was something odd about you. We'll be off again in a minute … got some spares to drop off up country and then back here. Fancy a ride?'

It was the best offer I'd had for some while, but I had barely said 'yes, please' when the flight engineer reported an engine snag and that was that.

In the morning – Day 3 – 'further instruction' had not arrived, but Doug and I had enjoyed a grand 'catch-up' in the bar. His engine had been fixed but the aircraft had developed a cracked windscreen panel, which put paid to his onward delivery and delayed his return to home base while his masters debated various solutions.

One of these was obvious to me.

'Do you think I could borrow you and your aircraft?' I suggested, only half in jest.

'That would be great, and we've probably got the right kit on board, but my flying category has expired. I was due an update back at base yesterday, but the delay means that now I'm technically not qualified. I'm not sure whether I can even take the aircraft home.'

And I thought I had problems!

On Day 4 everything was resolved for both of us. My exercise had been abandoned and I was to return to Malta as best I could. Doug was granted a special, one-off authority to fly his cracked aeroplane – crew only – at low-level back to Cyprus.

We parted at the Operations Centre.

'Great to see you again,' he said, warily eyeing my re-armed escort. 'See you 'round.'

Long after I had made my last parachute jump and Mike had hung up his goggles he insisted that we attend a private reunion at his place.

'It has to be these dates,' he said. 'The others can make it then.'

'What others?'

He would not say, but we sort-of guessed and on the day it was wonderful to find Doug and wife ensconced on the patio.

'Doug!' I cried. 'Just look at you … How long's it been?'

'I reckon 35 years,' Mike interrupted, and touched the elbow of a tall man with his back turned.

A moment's rushing through the memory banks, 'Gordon!'

'Well over 40,' Gordon admitted, with a strong grip.

On the following day – the women off base – four ageing warriors sat in the sun, drinking beer and swapping war stories.

'So how did you get all this together?' I asked Mike.

'Well… Gordon and I trained as pilots together, then kept in touch … Doug and I flew the same aircraft, then kept in touch … With me so far?'

'Yes, but I was the odd man out. I wasn't a pilot.'

'Ah… you were neighbours of Doug and me and jumped out of our aircraft.'

'Okay, so how does that link me and Gordon?'

'You went to school with Gordon and he recognised your name when I lent him a book.'

The circle was complete and we broached another beer in acknowledgement.

'One more loop to loop,' Mike continued, mischievously. 'I got this from the Retired List. While you and Gordon were probably born within a month or two of each other, the real dirt is that you and Doug were also probably born within twenty miles of each other, but…' he paused to sip his drink. 'On exactly the same day! How long's it been?'

19. SOMEBODY HAS TO PAY

For generations it is likely that none of us in the Services gave any thought whatever to the cost of doing our job. What did an hour or two's flying of an aircraft actually amount to in real money? How much did it cost to cut all the grass or to maintain a proper military presence? For those of us on the shop floor, it simply was not our business to know who actually paid the bills.

For sure, the conscientious commander might run an occasional campaign amongst his people and then would follow an earnest, but short-lived period of switching off lights, reducing vehicle use and perhaps – only *perhaps* – not requiring every form in triplicate.

Otherwise, unless holding a headquarters staff appointment with a moral duty to worry about these matters, everybody bumbled along, doing their bit in defence of the country – and if that cost somebody a lot, then that was the price to be paid.

And so it was until the late 1980s, when I was unexpectedly appointed in executive command of all support services at a medium-sized but busy station. Everything from estate management to personnel and transport to chaplaincy entered my orbit.

At our first meeting, my station commander bravely concealed his dismay at my lack of experience in the intricacies of Air Force administration.

'Simple pilots don't know these things,' he laughed, indicating his 'wings'. Then, pointing to my proudly-worn parachute badge, 'And I don't suppose *that's* going to help you either.'

Unfortunately, our harmonious survival – there were aeroplanes for him to fly and I headed a large admin staff (each expert in their own field) – was threatened by the introduction of a revolutionary accounting scheme across all three services.

Local commanders were to bid for funds to run their unit and a 'live' budget would be imposed as the personal responsibility of the CO and his senior executives. There was even a budget for everybody's pay. Overspends, it seemed, meant firing squads.

Naturally, the new scheme came complete with its very own acronyms. Stern instructions identified the principle as E.R.B and we were to employ a Civil Service E.R.B.O. – ours turned out to be a young, resilient and highly-trained management accountant. How easily her qualification rolled off the tongue, but I had not the first idea what it meant.

However, it seemed she would not actually count pennies.

Our 'Erbo' was to report directly to the station commander – through me – on how the 'Erb' was getting along. It was all very baffling for ordinary knockabout officers and calls to our personal secretary for more coffee became more frantic as we pored over the volumes of paperwork that presaged our fate. Much of this was in fax form – one being over 12 feet long (I measured it) and brought along more arcane expressions understood only by our masters: *Ring Fencing*, *Cost Centres* and *Outturns*.

Gradually the procedures settled into a fortnightly and massive spreadsheet that I was required to *sign-off* and thereafter remain personally liable for £25 million.

It was hard not to rush out there and then to switch off hangar floodlights or restrict the small arms range to ten bullets per shoot.

'Slightly over your pay band, perhaps?' quipped the boss.

'It's a funny thing,' I grumped. 'In previous incarnations our getting it wrong could have killed us. Now our failure will produce nagging by the bean counters … a worse fate by far.'

The Erbo valiantly attempted explanation, but often concluded apologetically by saying it was difficult even for specialists.

'But no,' I boasted. 'I actually made sense of something yesterday. Somebody has been travelling on the Norwegian State Railway. I'd like to know why.'

'Do you think you've got the measure of this?' my leader asked. 'It must be like nailing jelly to the wall.'

It was a perfect summary.

Before long, other, less respectful acronyms appeared. My CO particularly enjoyed one from the Army's jungle drums that identified the **S**pecial **H**igh **I**ntensity **T**raining that I was required to attend.

This, an 'executives' seminar', was to be held in a four-star hotel at a five-star yacht marina, thereby making the business of prudent unit budgeting difficult to reconcile.

My fellow students – Navy, Army and Air Force – were as baffled as me. Most had recently been appointed into administrative functions from operational appointments. None of us had the required background, training or – we ruefully confessed – inclination, so our civilian mentors quickly wearied of our comparisons with riding a tank, a frigate or a parachute.

Saddest by far was a civilian librarian, from a highly sensitive weapons establishment, presumably full of very expensive bombs. He seemingly had just been passing his boss's door at the wrong moment.

All was not lost, however. In our midst was an Army Pay Corps major; a fully-trained management accountant. He would keep us on the right track – our tutors' eyes lit up – but during the first coffee break even he declared bewilderment.

At the end of it all, still unconverted, I waited for my train, in company with another who was facing a longish journey. He was a pilot, but now, like me, serving his first 'admin' tour of duty. The morning headlines shouted in huge letters that the opening air strikes of the First Gulf War had been mounted.

'Let's hope the chaps don't exceed their budgets,' we said as one … and took our perplexity home.

'Never mind the Gulf…' was the welcome home from my boss. 'The real news is that your budget woman ploughed her final exams while you were away. Now we … meaning you … will have to fund her to have another go.'

Two weeks later, to celebrate her eventual success, the Erbo brought really dire news. The sneaky bounder who had been buying Norwegian railway tickets did not exist; that expenditure had been at another unit and wrongly attributed to us.

'It was the central computer, you know.'

I was distraught. Gone from my gigantic spreadsheet was the only piece of information I recognised, together with my stick for beating the many spendthrifts about the place.

Months passed, and gradually everything settled down, until one day the Erbo came in, grave of face.

'Morning sir.' This sounded ominous; as a civilian she rarely used the military greeting. 'Good news or bad?'

'Oh dear, let's try the bad.'

'Well, I'll not mess about. You are two million adrift.'

Suddenly, Iraq really was a long way away.

'Over or under?' I squeaked.

'Oh ... under, of course. The good news is that I'm pretty sure you're not responsible. It's something to do with the pay budget of a unit that moved out en bloc three months ago. The central computer ... yes, that again ... has not adjusted yet.'

'Good news or bad?' I offered my station commander over morning coffee.

'Bad,' he grinned. 'I've got my own good news.'

'We've got a two million deficit on the dreaded budget.'

'Only two million?' He spread his hands philosophically. 'I thought you were going to say a few hundred. If we're going to go down, let's do it in style. And now my news...'

He pushed over a single sheet of paper.

'I've been doing my own sums.'

More mischievous grins.

'Because of your seniority and parachute pay, you cost my budget much more than a younger man would.'

I glanced at the paper.

The end of my tour of duty was imminent and this was formal notice of my next appointment.

'Let's hope your successor is a *real* administrator who knows what he is doing, but I doubt if it will be as much fun.'

'Steady on ... you call this *fun?*'

As was only proper, the boss had the last word.

'As for the lost millions ... I have no choice ... you're fired!'

20. LEST I FORGET

My generation of military men and women served our time supposedly in peacetime, even though there was enough going on to belie that condition: Oman, Aden, the Falklands, Northern Ireland. Thankfully, the ever-present Cold War never became 'hot' in any large-scale way.

History may show us to have been lucky – considering what is required of our forces today – but the training and preparation to counter Soviet adventures in Europe kept most of us fully occupied throughout our careers.

We followed the time-honoured Service ethos that, in war or peace, the show must go on – we'll argue about the detail and the politics afterwards, but only when we have time to draw breath.

For me, during repeated returns to the specialised world of military parachute training, the dangers of the work, though routinely denied, would come to the fore at regular intervals. A clear uneventful period – sometimes many years – would be followed by two or even three fatal incidents in short order.

We were a small unit, the only one of its type in the RAF, and matters could become a bit 'tribal', but after serious accidents the immediate reaction would be a wake in honour – *it might be me tomorrow.* The enquiries and brooding would come later.

Then we continued our trust in reliable equipment, proven procedure – both possibly amended – and a highly-disciplined, optimistic professionalism; no different to any other military unit, really.

All this came home to me shortly after I had left the parachuting world – I had still been jumping in my 50th year – and when I attended an All Souls ceremony in the nearby town cemetery.

The Polish ex-pat community were to honour their dead of World War Two and rejuvenate the hope that the imminent independence of their country would restore easy contact with their extended families. In uniform, I was to represent my station, which had a wartime Polish history, and pay tribute at the memorial.

My driver set me down at the gates and, as I marched up the avenue towards the cenotaph, I saw the gathered heads and then heard their voices in song.

Evidently, proceedings had begun.

'I'll do that PA,' I vowed. 'She's misread the programme timings.'

I hurried on and inserted myself into the crowd as unobtrusively as possible. Next to me was the Lady Mayor, in full scarlet fig, lace at the neck, Mace Bearer and all.

I raised my eyebrows in abject apology.

Nobody else looked towards us and I had barely settled when another RAF officer, who I recognised from a neighbouring station, crept up beside me. We nodded in silent recognition and gestured towards the memorial cross with our poppy wreaths.

Surely, two PAs could not be wrong?

Under a dire east wind, direct from Siberia via the Lincolnshire Fens, the congregation chanted a series of mournful dirges, entirely in Polish, and I fell to my own reflecting.

The aircraft crash, along with the aircrew and all trainee parachutists on board, had taken eight instructors from my small unit...

On my right, the Mayor's attendant was handing her a large wreath.

An NCO colleague – we had trained together as instructors – had been on board an aircraft that flew into the sea.

The proud Polish keening faltered not a note.

Two staff members killed in an aircraft that crashed on take-off. Then the survivors' wives' disbelief as I sought to belie the horrific scene shown on the TV news.

The east wind was chilling my bones, while half an ear had taken in progress at the ceremony. Suddenly I recognised the English names of the town, my station and that of my neighbour. It was time to follow the Mayor, lay our wreaths and salute.

It was the same compliment given at the grave of a young officer killed in a parachute accident not long before. We had formed up while a large transport aircraft, crabbing sideways in a huge crosswind, dipped towards us in salute. I had taken the news of his death from a tight-lipped warrant officer who, stiff with formality, had volunteered to meet me at Heathrow and escort me carefully back to my unit.

I blamed myself for persuading the young man to become a parachute instructor in the first place, but had no answer to the anger of a colleague who, on the fateful day, after having jumped together, watched the continued fall from under his safely-opened parachute.

The Poles had ended their tribute and with brief hand-shakes were dispersing quickly. We two RAF officers made to apologise to the Mayor for our disrespectful lateness.

'No need for apologies,' she replied. 'I was only minutes ahead of you myself. You see, the Poles gathered early, and when *they* were all here, they began.'

It was a gracious let-out. They were right; we were mere bit-players in this context. We might not have been missed, but it would have been unforgivable to have turned away.

It was my last formal memorial service in uniform, but because of the incomprehensible language, the aching weather and my time in service, the most moving of all I had attended.

Now it is time to visit the Armed Forces Memorial in Staffordshire. There will be no need to search for names; they are all there – permanently.

~ END ~